# PRAIS
# TOUCHED
# TRANSFORMED

*Touched and Transformed* reaches into the depths of soul pain. It has nothing of the world's ineffectual Band-Aids, which serve only to hide wounds, not heal them. In Jeremiah 6:14 God warns against "superficial healing" and gives the one true remedy for every human distress or deprivation, and that is to return to the only One who can heal the deepest pain with a love that goes deeper still.

**Margaret Ashmore**
Denton Bible Church
Denton, Texas

We have discovered understanding the names and character of God to be one of the most important means to both emotional and spiritual well-being. As Sally states in the introduction, "First we must be willing to come to Him." Knowing His names promotes in us a desire to do that, allowing Him to lead us in triumph rather than defeat.

**Pastor Dale and Cathy Dickinson**
Jericho Road Christian Fellowship
El Cajon, California

*Touched and Transformed* brings hope to those who have tried to fill the emptiness in their lives as a result of hurts from the past. *Touched and Transformed* leads the reader to what the hurting need: God and all His promises. It reveals a love beyond anything ever known that can heal and transform lives in a mighty way as people receive the power of God's Spirit! The reader will find who they have needed all along: Jesus, *Jehovah Shalom*.

**Colleen Hughes**
Domestic violence and sexual assault advocate
Riverside County, California

# TOUCHED & TRANSFORMED

## HOPE FOR THE HURTING
### A NINE-WEEK DISCIPLESHIP STUDY

*When Jesus saw him lying there,*
*and knew that he already had been in that condition a long time,*
*He said to him, "Do you want to be made well?"*
John 5:6

# SALLY VAN WICK

Touched and Transformed: Hope for the Hurting

Published by Sally Van Wick

Temecula, California, U.S.A.

Printed in the U.S.A.

ISBN-13: 978-0-9983927-0-7

For additional information please visit sallyvanwick.com, e-mail sally@ccbf.net, or write to 34180 Rancho California Road, Temecula, CA 92591, U.S.A.

Cover and interior design by Five J's Design | fivejsdesign.com

Cover photo: Lightstock | Pearl

# CONTENTS

# FOREWORD

## BRIAN AND CHERYL BRODERSEN

The old hymn asks, "Would you be free from your burden of sin?" It then answers this question with the remedy for that emancipation: "There is power, power, wonder working power in the precious blood of the Lamb." In the course of ministry, we have had the opportunity to meet and minister to many people who struggle to appropriate this emancipating power of Jesus in their lives. Though they are Christians, they continue to struggle with the shame, condemnation, emotional pain, and torment of events from their pasts.

A few years ago Sally Van Wick shared with us how she was endeavoring to minister to Christians who needed to be delivered and healed from the damage caused by past trauma. These believers had tried programs, methods, and counseling programs but had not met with success. Sally recognized that the healing she and her husband, Clark, had found in their own lives had come as they began to truly know the character and love of God. As their understanding deepened, not only had their wounds healed but a desire to bring this divine healing to others had manifested itself in Sally's heart. Somewhat frustrated with manuals that promised healing but drew more attention to the past hurts than the present reality of God's great power, Sally began to feel the Spirit's leading to write her own workbook.

Each time we met up with Sally and Clark, we inquired about how the book was coming. The process was slow but sure. Each chapter was thought out carefully, prayed over diligently, and written from the heart.

*Touched and Transformed* is the fruit of that labor of love. The focus of this book is the person of God as He has revealed Himself in Scripture. The Bible is God's revelation of His power, love, and grace for humanity.

We are confident that those who take the journey through *Touched and Transformed* will be touched and transformed by appropriating the truths of the holy God who created them, loved them to the greatest depths by sending His only Son to save them, and delights to manifest His healing grace to all who receive Him.

Are you ready to be touched by God? Are you willing to be free of those ghastly torments of the past that constantly spoil your best moments? If so, prepare to be transformed by the transforming truths you will find as you learn to appropriate the character of God in your heart and mind.

The Bible promises that God will draw near to those who draw near to Him (see James 4:8). We pray that as you draw near to God through *Touched and Transformed*, God will indeed draw near to you, touching and transforming your life. Get ready to be set free!

# PREFACE

Every one of us has experienced pain. The problem is, too many of us carry our pain with us, buried deep inside, and never find the healing that God intends us to have.

Perhaps you've been divorced. Maybe you feel as if you married the wrong person. Your child may have been aborted or miscarried. Maybe you were sexually or physically assaulted or emotionally abused and have kept it a secret for a long time. Or perhaps someone has falsely accused you of abuse or some other wrong and you have a hard time forgiving that person.

Maybe you have a difficult relationship with your mother, your father, or a sibling. Maybe one of your parents abused you as a child. Perhaps you don't feel safe in your home.

You may have received care from a doctor or counselor, or you may have avoided professional help. Perhaps you are filled with pain but can't bring yourself to tell anyone or ask for help. Maybe you long for peace but have no idea how to resolve the issues that plague you.

You may be part of a church, or perhaps you never darken the door of God's house. You may read the Bible, pray, have family devotions, and perhaps even be involved in ministry in your church, or perhaps you find it hard to pray or draw near to God. Maybe you know that God loves you, but you don't love Him.

As a pastor's wife and Bible-study teacher at Calvary Chapel Bible Fellowship in Temecula, California, I meet men and women every day who carry heavy baggage from their pasts. I have been one of those people, so it's easy for me to spot them! Millions of men and women suffer from emotional wounds from past events such as abandonment, betrayal, rape, neglect, or the loss of a loved one. These life occurrences can cause paralyzing depression, self-destruction, dependence on drugs, and other damaging effects. Regardless of their cause, these wounds affect not only the person suffering from them but also that person's relationships with others.

This is why I wrote *Touched and Transformed*. In my years of ministry, I have seen hurting people try study after study, trying to find some answer to the pain they are carrying in their lives. I hope this study will be different. I hope it will point people to Jesus Christ, the living Word of God—the only One who can reveal the root of each person's pain and lead them to true and lasting healing.

*Touched and Transformed* is a nine-week study, with each week containing five daily lessons. After each day's reading you will be asked to answer questions relating to the life circumstances of various Bible characters in order to discover how God worked His purpose for His glory in each one's specific situation. On the last day of each week's study, you will become familiar with some of the many names of God, learning more about His character and promises and how those relate to your life. Throughout the study you will want to come to the Lord with an open, transparent heart ready to receive.

At our church we pair each person who uses *Touched and Transformed* with a leader, someone prayerfully chosen who takes the person's situation seriously and desires to point him or her to the "God of all comfort" (2 Cor. 1:3). The leader's main objective is to encourage an individual to seek a closer relationship with Jesus so that the person will know Him more and, in that knowledge, be free to "grow in the grace and knowledge of our Lord and Savior Jesus Christ" (2 Pet. 3:18). If you choose to do the study with a leader, know that it is vital to be open and honest in sharing your past hurts, but in order to do this, it is important to ask a pastor or church leader to help you find a trustworthy, godly person who can be trusted to treat your past hurts with sensitivity, understanding, and confidentiality. But while pairing individuals with a leader is an ideal format for our church,

*Touched and Transformed* can be used by churches, ministries, groups, or individuals in any way that works best for them.

This biblical discipleship ministry for people dealing with painful unresolved issues, both men and women, is not directed toward any one issue but instead focuses on the character of God and His divine influence upon the hearts of His people.

*Touched and Transformed* encourages participants to meet directly with God so that they might know His unconditional love and trust Him for true healing. God is able to supernaturally change lives by His grace, and I pray that each person who goes through this study would prayerfully seek God's transforming work to receive the freedom that comes only from His touch.

My prayer is that through this study you will recognize the root of these deep issues and allow God to heal the wounded areas of your heart.

# A Note from
# Pastor Clark Van Wick

Sally and I are truly humbled and honored to have the opportunity to serve the body of Christ at Calvary Chapel Bible Fellowship. More than anything, we want others to know the love and goodness of God and the freedom that is found in the grace of Jesus.

We are often confronted with men and women whose problems seem to be based on past or present issues that have not been dealt with appropriately according to the Word of God.

Sally and I both saw the need for a biblically based tool to help guide people to the Lord's healing touch and a true understanding of His character. Through much prayer, I encouraged Sally to create a discipleship study to help men and women grow in His grace.

It's so important to understand that the Word of God relates directly to our lives today regardless of our gender or age—that's what makes *Touched and Transformed* so uniquely powerful. This study walks the reader through the Word of God with a focus on biblical testimonies and on the names and character of God. Through *Touched and Transformed* people's lives will be changed as they are brought into a deeper understanding of the Lord, based completely upon His Word, as His Spirit creates a renewed hunger in them to know Him relationally.

Jesus offers hope for the hurting and healing for the brokenhearted—to those who want to be made well. There is no other way to find rest for our souls apart from Jesus. I highly recommend *Touched and Transformed* to anyone who is seeking a complete healing; no matter who you are or what your past or present holds, Jesus is the answer.

I thank God for allowing us to be a part of the work He is doing, and I look forward to seeing all He will continue to do through *Touched and Transformed*.

By His grace,
Pastor Clark Van Wick

# ACKNOWLEDGMENTS

Special thanks from the depth of my heart to

Jesus: I am so thankful to Jesus Christ for saving me. He took me from a life of sin and destruction. He touched me with the power of His Holy Spirit and forever transformed my life through His comfort, healing, and restoration as only He can do.

My parents: I would like to thank my wonderful parents for their sacrifice, love, and patience through my difficult years growing up and for always being there for me.

My church family: I want to give a special thanks to all who gave insight and inspiration and prayed for this project.

Jeff and Lori Wear, Teresa Dodson, Barb Price, Melissa Landis, Andrea Archambeau, Tim and Beth Watkins, Pastor Ricco Gomez, and others: thank you for committing hours of service guiding others to Jesus as He touches and transforms their lives through this study.

Rob and Kim Thompson and Emily Barton: thank you for helping with the initial edit and organization.

Cheryl Brodersen: thank you, my friend, for the encouragement and example of what it means to live a life committed to Jesus in every aspect!

My editor, Becky English: thank you; it was a pleasure working with you. I definitely could not have done this without you!

My proofreader, Jennifer Cullis, and my designers, Jeff and Joy Miller of Five J's Design: thank you for your excellent work on the manuscript and on the interior, cover, and e-book designs.

And last but definitely not least, Pastor Clark Van Wick: I especially want to thank my incredible husband, who is my pastor, boss, best friend, encourager, and mentor. You are an incredible father to our children and amazing grandfather to our grandchildren. Thank you for loving me with the love of Jesus through the messes I made of my life before I came to Christ. You are an incredible example of what it is to be a man after God's heart. I love you so much!

# Week 1
## Touched and Transformed—Healing in Jesus

*Do not be conformed to this world, but be transformed by the renewing of your mind, that you may prove what is that good and acceptable and perfect will of God.*

Romans 12:2

### DAY 1: HEALING—PAINFUL BUT REWARDING

When I was young and just learning to ride a bicycle, I rounded a corner too fast and fell, badly scraping my leg. Because asphalt was imbedded in my skin, my mother had to scrub the wound until the dirt and gravel were removed. The process was extremely painful, but my mother told me that if I wanted the wound to heal properly, the impurities had to be cleaned out.

It is much the same with people's hearts. In order for healing to take place in our lives from the hurts we have inevitably experienced, we must allow God to cleanse our heart wounds so that the infection of bitterness doesn't set in.

This begins by acknowledging the sin associated with our wounds—*whether it is our own sin or another's that has affected us.* This process of addressing our wounds and the sin that has caused them can be very painful, but it is necessary, and the rewards for those who persevere in it will be immeasurable. As you work through *Touched and Transformed*, you may be tempted to stop when the journey becomes too painful, but be encouraged by Philippians 1:6: "Being confident of this very thing, that He who has begun a good work in you will complete it until the day of Jesus Christ." The Lord wants to bring you real and lasting healing.

The problem is, we tend to carry our past pain with us. But doing this is like choosing to carry trash around. Who places their trash on the curb only to run after the garbage truck asking for their bags back? Probably no one! Yet how often do we do that in our lives? We give God the sins or hurts that have wounded us, but before we know it, we go back to pick up the "garbage" we've left behind. The longer we carry it with us, however, the more it stinks; and the more garbage we choose to carry, the worse the odor becomes. While we can grow accustomed to the stench, others around us are negatively affected by it.

Just as the garbage man removes our garbage completely, so God promises us in Psalm 103:12 that "as far as the east is from the west, so far has He removed our transgressions from us." As we choose to truly surrender our past hurts and pain to Jesus and seek His healing, the sweet fragrance of Christ will begin to come forth from our lives and then draw others to Him: "Thanks be to God who always leads us in triumph in Christ, and through us diffuses the fragrance of His knowledge in every place. For we are to God the fragrance of Christ among those who are being saved and among those who are perishing" (2 Cor. 2:14–15).

But first we must be willing to come to Him, trusting Him to remove the garbage from our past and give us His healing in return. Today is the day! Choose what you want to emanate from your life—the stench of your past or the fragrance of Christ.

As you consider the need to face painful things in order to gain healing in your life, answer the questions below.

1. Have you ever looked squarely at your own sin or the sin of others toward you in order to find healing? How willing are you to do so? Write your thoughts below.

2. What "garbage" from your past might you be carrying with you? How has this affected you over the months and years?

## DAY 2: THE SOLUTION—JESUS CHRIST

Jesus gives us an invitation in Matthew 11:28–30: "Come to Me, all you who labor and are heavy laden, and I will give you rest. Take My yoke upon you and learn from Me, for I am gentle and lowly in heart, and you will find rest for your souls. For My yoke is easy and My burden is light." He is calling you today.

Jesus came "to seek and save that which was lost" (Luke 19:10). He also came that we may have life and that we may have it more abundantly (see John 10:10). In Jeremiah 29:11–13 God tells us, "I know the thoughts that I think toward you, says the LORD, thoughts of peace and not of evil, to give you a future and a hope. Then you will call upon Me and go and pray to Me, and I will listen to you. And you will seek Me and find Me, when you search for Me with all your heart." If you will seek Him, you *will* find Him and get to know Him. Call upon Jesus, and come to Him with an open heart, seeking to know Him more intimately. Let Him speak into the deep places of your life with words of comfort and healing.

*Touched and Transformed* is not a superficial Band-Aid to cover over wounds but an introduction to the all-sufficient, all-satisfying God of the universe, the only One who can truly transform our lives. He has not called us to religion or to *things we must do* but to a love relationship with Himself because of *what He has already done.* We don't need to clean ourselves up to come to Him; we can simply come as we are and ask Him to do the work that only He can do in our lives.

God's love is not based on our performance; rather, it is unconditional and undeserved. There is nothing we can do to earn it and nothing we can do to stop it. Jesus loves us in spite of our disobedience, weakness, sin, and selfishness. One of the most powerful scriptures, Romans 5:8, shows us this: "God demonstrates His own love toward us, in that while we were still sinners, Christ died for us." God loves us so much that He sent His Son to die on the cross for us that we might have everlasting life with Him. His work is complete, and now we can simply rest in His great love for us. He did this so that we would "know the love of Christ which passes knowledge" and "be filled with all the fullness of God" (Eph. 3:19).

When we are hurting or dealing with a difficult situation, it is easy to believe the lie that no one understands what we are going through. While it's true that not everyone understands our feelings at any given moment, we can be assured that Jesus understands our hearts perfectly.

While not everyone understands what we are going through, some people *can* relate to the issues we have experienced. Throughout *Touched and Transformed* we will look at biblical characters such as David, Hannah, Solomon, Joseph, and others who struggled with wounds of the heart. God used these men and women in mighty ways even as they suffered abandonment, abuse, neglect, and betrayal as well as poor choices that carried dire consequences. When we read God's Word, we can relate to the lives of these people who, despite their varying circumstances, had one thing in common: faith in an incredible God who always worked things out for His glory far better than they could ever have expected or imagined.

In 2 Corinthians 1:3–5 we read, "Blessed be the God and Father of our Lord Jesus Christ, the Father of mercies and God of all comfort, who comforts us in all our tribulation, that we may be able to comfort those who are in any trouble, with the comfort with which we ourselves are comforted by God. For as the sufferings of Christ abound in us, so our consolation also abounds through Christ." The Bible assures us that we are never alone. Not only does God understand our issues, but He also sympathizes with our weaknesses (see Heb. 4:15) and promises us His comforting presence in the midst of our situations.

*We do not have a High Priest who cannot sympathize with our weaknesses, but was in all points tempted as we are, yet without sin.*

Hebrews 4:15

1. How is God calling you regarding your need for healing? What is He saying to you specifically right now?

2. The Bible is not a book about perfect people but about men and women who have walked through incredible challenges, some of their own making and some through the cruelty of others. How

encouraging is it to you that people in the Bible have gone through things that you may be dealing with today?

## DAY 3: TAKING SPIRITUAL INVENTORY

The prophet Jeremiah likens our lives to that of a tree:

> Blessed is the man who trusts in the LORD, and whose hope is the LORD. For he shall be like a tree planted by the waters, which spreads out its roots by the river, and will not fear when heat comes; but its leaf will be green, and will not be anxious in the year of drought, nor will cease from yielding fruit. (Jer. 17:7–8)

He compares the roots to our belief system and the fruit to our choices, actions, emotions, attitudes, and relationships with God and others. In other words, *what we believe* is at the root of the fruit produced in and through our lives. If we have a healthy root system, our lives will yield healthy fruit. A. W. Tozer, one of my favorite authors, states in his book *The Root of the Righteous*, "A tree can weather almost any storm if its root is sound,"[1] and he quotes from Proverbs 12:12: "The root of the righteous yields fruit." If we want healthy fruit in our lives, we must be rooted in the truth of God's Word: "The entirety of Your word is truth, and every one of Your righteous judgments endures forever" (Ps. 119:160).

*Abide in Me, and I in you. As the branch cannot bear fruit of itself, unless it abides in the vine, neither can you, unless you abide in Me.*

**John 15:4**

We don't have to work for fruit. As we simply become rooted and grounded in God's truth, He naturally produces good and pleasing fruit in our lives. Galatians 5:22–23 explains, "The fruit of the Spirit is love, joy, peace, longsuffering, kindness, goodness, faithfulness, gentleness, self-control. Against such there is no law."

On the other hand, when we believe lies and thus choose not to do things God's way, bad fruit is produced. Tozer also wrote, "Wrong beliefs will stop the growth of any Christian life. Wrong desire perverts the moral judgment so that we are unable to appraise the desired object at its real value."[2] If we fail to believe the truth of who God is and instead place our trust in man, the result will be disastrous: "Cursed is the man who trusts in man and makes flesh his strength, whose heart departs from the Lord. For he shall be like a shrub in the desert, and shall not see when good comes, but shall inhabit the parched places in the wilderness, in a salt land which is not inhabited" (Jer. 17:5–6).

Jesus teaches us that Satan is the originator of lies, and these lies are at the root of bad fruit. In John 8:44 Jesus tells those who did not believe in Him, "You are of your father the devil, and the desires of your father you want to do. He was a murderer from the beginning, and does not stand in the truth, because there is no truth in him. When he speaks a lie, he speaks from his own resources, for he is a liar and the father of it." Whether we are a believer or a non-believer, when we believe Satan's lies, they will have control over our lives, and we will produce bad fruit.

What kind of fruit are you producing? Read through the following list, circling any symptom that is being manifested in your life:

Abusing others

Abstinence/lack of sexual interest

Anger/rage

Anxiety/anguish

Avoidance of personal relationships

Bitterness

Busyness

Comparison of yourself to others

Condemnation/feeling dirty

Confusion

Controlling others

Cutting (self-abuse)

Depression

Despair

Drawing attention to yourself

Eating disorder

Emotional numbness

Fear of failure

Fear of God's punishment

Fear of losing a child

Fear of any further relationships

Fear of pregnancy/infertility

Feeling degraded/debased

Feeling inferior

Feeling rejected

Feeling exploited

Flashbacks or nightmares

Frustration

Grief/sorrow

Guilt

Helplessness

Hopelessness

Horror

Inability to bond with living children, spouse, or others

Inability to forgive

Inability to receive forgiveness

Isolation

Loneliness

Believing you are not loved

Obsessive behaviors

Over-protectiveness

Panic

Paranoia

Perfectionism

Regret/remorse

Revenge

Sabotaging healthy relationships

Self-doubt

Self-hatred

Self-pity

Sense of victimization—desiring pity

Sexual promiscuity

Shame

Social anxiety

Substance abuse

Unworthiness

Wounding others

Now look at this second list, and circle any triggers that cause the above symptoms to manifest:

Events/anniversaries

Conversations

Holidays

Movies/visuals

Places

Seasons

Sensitive subjects

Smells

Sounds/songs

Touches/gestures

*As you have therefore received Christ Jesus the Lord, so walk in Him, rooted and built up in Him and established in the faith, as you have been taught, abounding in it with thanksgiving.*

*Beware lest anyone cheat you through philosophy and empty deceit, according to the tradition of men, according to the basic principles of the world, and not according to Christ. For in Him dwells all the fullness of the Godhead bodily; and you are complete in Him, who is the head of all principality and power.*

**Colossians 2:6–10**

Galatians 5:17 tells us that "the flesh lusts against the Spirit, and the Spirit against the flesh; and these are contrary to one another, so that you do not do the things that you wish." Galatians 6:7–8 further states, "Whatever a man sows, that he will also reap. For he who sows to his flesh will of the flesh reap corruption, but he who sows to the Spirit will of the Spirit reap everlasting life." It is essential to recognize the war that is going on between the

Spirit and our flesh. Just as a tree draws its nourishment from the water and soil that surrounds it, so we draw from what surrounds us, whether what is true—the Word of God through the Spirit—or the lies of the enemy and the desires of our flesh.

This analogy of a tree shows why it is good for us to take spiritual inventory and ask ourselves: "What is it about my past experiences or relationships that has caused me to view God in a wrong way and believe lies?" We must only allow what God says about us in His Word to define us. Neither past experiences nor the enemy can determine our true value and worth.

*The LORD will guide you continually, and satisfy your soul in drought, and strengthen your bones; you shall be like a watered garden, and like a spring of water, whose waters do not fail.*
**Isaiah 58:11**

It always comes down to asking ourselves:

• What is my view of God?

• What is my relationship with God?

• What truth do I believe about God?

• Will I trust God?

• What does God say about who I am?

In light of the questions above, take a few minutes to ask yourself the following questions and consider what you actually believe. Do you believe that . . .

1. God exists? "Without faith it is impossible to please Him, for he who comes to God must believe that He is, and that He is a rewarder of those who diligently seek Him" (Heb. 11:6).

2. God is all-powerful? "God is exalted by His power;

28

who teaches like Him? Who has assigned Him His way, or who has said, 'You have done wrong'? Remember to magnify His work, of which men have sung. Everyone has seen it; man looks on it from afar" (Job 36:22–25).

3. God is good? "The Lord is gracious and full of compassion, slow to anger and great in mercy. The Lord is good to all, and His tender mercies are over all His works" (Ps. 145:8–9).

4. God loves you unconditionally? "Greater love has no one than this, than to lay down one's life for his friends" (John 15:13).

5. God promises us He is going to cause all things to come together for good? "We know that all things work together for good to those who love God, to those who are the called according to His purpose" (Rom. 8:28).

6. God created us with purpose and meaning? "I know the thoughts that I think toward you, says the Lord, thoughts of peace and not of evil, to give you a future and a hope. Then you will call upon Me and go and pray to Me, and I will listen to you. And you will seek Me and find Me, when you search for Me with all your heart" (Jer. 29:11–13).

7. We must choose to seek Him? "I call heaven and earth as witnesses today against you, that I have set before you life and death, blessing and cursing; therefore choose life, that both you and your descendants may live; that you may love the

Lord your God, that you may obey His voice, and that you may cling to Him, for He is your life and the length of your days; and that you may dwell in the land which the Lord swore to your fathers, to Abraham, Isaac, and Jacob, to give them" (Deut. 30:19–20).

8. Upon repentance we are forgiven? "If we confess our sins, He is faithful and just to forgive us our sins and to cleanse us from all unrighteousness" (1 John 1:9).

Our goal is never simply to change outward behavior for the sake of looking good to others but rather to allow the Spirit to change us from the inside out. When we try to ignore or cut off bad fruit after it is produced, we are not dealing with the root of the problem—the lie that is hidden. Behavior modification rarely, if ever, produces real, lasting results. True healing must start at the root.

*The root of the righteous yields fruit.*
**Proverbs 12:12**

But remember, God is gentle and loving. He doesn't uproot the broken areas of our lives to hurt us, but He gently uncovers the soil of any bad roots, trimming away the dead areas and pouring out the living water of His Word upon us for nourishment. We can trust Him to remove our damaged roots and give us new life and abiding fruit as we feed on His truth.

## DAY 4: DO YOU WANT TO BE MADE WELL?

Before any of us can be healed, we need to ask ourselves an important question: "Do I want to be made well?" The decision to be healed is a choice we must make, because God will never force Himself upon us. We must acknowledge the truth about ourselves and about God so that Jesus can touch and transform our lives.

Jeremiah 42:6 reveals the attitude that is necessary as we approach the Scriptures: "Whether it is pleasing or displeasing, we will obey the voice of the LORD our God to whom we send you, that it may be well with us when we obey the voice of the LORD our God." Do you truly want to be made well? Will you obey the voice of the Lord even if it is displeasing to you or makes you uncomfortable? We must choose to commit ourselves to Him on a daily basis, sometimes moment by moment, trusting Him with our healing process.

*Search me, O God, and know my heart; try me, and know my anxieties; and see if there is any wicked way in me, and lead me in the way everlasting.*
**Psalm 139:23–24**

To facilitate healing, learning to develop a quiet time with the Lord through His Word is essential. A relationship with anyone involves a commitment of time and communication, and it is the same in our relationship with Jesus. As we surrender our lives to Him, He will give us His Spirit to guide us and direct our paths.

But a quiet time with God is not about how much we read or pray; it's about how much we seek Him and respond to Him. May we never open our Bibles or pray without truly seeking Jesus with all our hearts, minds, and souls. As we seek *Him* and hold on to His promises, we will find that He will be faithful to complete what He has begun in our lives, healing our hearts and leading us in victory—all for His glory.

*You will seek Me and find Me, when you search for Me with all your heart.*
**Jeremiah 29:13**

To develop a quiet time with the Lord, find a place where you can be alone each day with the Lord and your

Bible. Ask the Holy Spirit to reveal Himself to you as you read a portion of His Word, keeping in mind the following:

What do I learn about

- God/Jesus/the Holy Spirit?

- The lies of Satan?

- My situation?

- Myself/my beliefs?

- The truth of God's Word?

Is there

- A command or example in the passage for me to follow?

- A false identity I need to confess?

- A lie that needs replacing with God's truth?

- Something I need to repent of?

- A sin or judgment I need to avoid?

- Something I need to surrender and trust God with?

When we take time to wait on the Lord, He hears our cries to Him and meets our needs: "I waited patiently for the LORD: and He inclined to me, and heard my cry. He also brought me up out of a horrible pit, out of the miry clay, and set my feet upon a rock, and established my steps. He has put a new song in my mouth—praise to our God; many will see it and fear, and will trust in the LORD" (Ps. 40:1–3).

1. How often do you seek the Lord in prayer and in His Word? What practical things can you do to help make this a regular habit in your life (get up earlier, find a quiet space away from others, set a timer, etc.)?

2. What do you believe you could gain by spending time with the Lord each day?

## DAY 5: SEEING JESUS IN THE NAMES OF GOD

There is a big difference between knowing *about* someone and knowing that person intimately. Just because we acknowledge someone's name doesn't mean we can trust or be transparent with that person. Take married people, for instance. If we only know *about* our spouses, we will not have much of a relationship with them; but as we get to *know* our spouses' character and respond to what pleases them, the marriage relationship will grow and be strengthened. It is the same with Jesus. The more we get to know Him and His character, the more we will respond to Him openly and honestly, trusting Him with our lives.

*Trust in the LORD with all your heart, and lean not on your own understanding; in all your ways acknowledge Him, and He shall direct your paths.*

**Proverbs 3:5–6**

How do we get to know Christ's character? God reveals it to us through His names as recorded in Scripture. Throughout *Touched and Transformed* we will study many of the different names of God. In biblical times a name often linked a person to a particular family lineage, occupation, calling, or predominant character trait. In much the same way, God's names yield a rich understanding of who He is, which in turn helps as we go through trials and difficulties in our lives.

Knowing the Lord's names gives us special insight into the person and promises of God and how He relates to our lives. For instance, knowing that God's name is *Jehovah Shammah*, meaning that He is with us, is comforting during times when we feel alone. Not only does the awareness of His presence reassure us, but it also reminds us that He sees everything we are going through. We also learn that nothing escapes His notice, because His name is *El Roi*, "the God who sees." Once we know God's true nature, we will trust Him more fully, and when we are able to trust Him, we can receive His healing touch. Getting to know God through His names truly transforms our lives.

When we know God's nature, it answers many of our

questions, such as, who is God? Whom can I trust? With whom can I be transparent? Who will never betray me? Who is this God who can take my ashes and turn them into something beautiful? Who sees me at all times? Who is with me no matter where I go? Who is jealous for my affection? Who came in the form of a man to take away my sin and redeem me eternally? Who alone can satisfy my thirsty soul? The answers to these questions and more are revealed as we get to know God through His names.

*Those who know Your name will put their trust in You; for You, LORD, have not forsaken those who seek You.*

**Psalm 9:10**

Knowing the names of God is a powerful tool against the enemy. When Satan whispers lies in our ear, we must always fall back to what we know to be true of God. When we focus on the name, character, and promises of God, we receive deliverance as we realize that our God is greater than any circumstance we find ourselves in. Then, as we are filled with His Spirit (we will discuss this in detail in week 9), we are given God's resurrection power, which enables us to go forth in the power and victory of the finished work of Jesus. When we are tempted to give in to the feeling that God does not care about us in our situations, we must remember His names.

The most valuable aspect of studying the Word of God is learning the truth about who God is and getting to know Him intimately. We can have many wrong ideas about God, but as we learn His names through His Word, we can be assured of His true character, His attributes, and also His promises, and this will give us confidence to call upon Him in times of trouble.

1. Think of someone you know only *about*, and then think of someone you *know*. What is the difference in your relationships with these two individuals?

2. How many names of God can you think of that you already know? Based on this, how well do you think you know the Lord?

As you spend time with the Lord Jesus Christ through *Touched and Transformed* and get to know Him better, it is my prayer that you will experience God's character in a truly transforming way and know His love like never before. As your hope is renewed and your faith strengthened, I pray that you will be not only healed of any pain that weighs you down but also equipped to reach out and help others with the help you will receive from Him. Above all, I pray that you will "know the love of Christ which passes knowledge; that you may be filled with all the fullness of God.

"Now to Him who is able to do exceedingly abundantly above all that we ask or think, according to the power that works in us, to Him be glory in the church by Christ Jesus to all generations, forever and ever. Amen" (Eph. 3:19–21).

# TOUCHED AND TRANSFORMED TO QUENCH OUR THIRST

*Jesus stood and cried out, saying, "If anyone thirsts, let him come to Me and drink. He who believes in Me, as the Scripture has said, out of his heart will flow rivers of living water."*

John 7:37–38

## DAY 1: WE ALL THIRST

En Gedi, located in the Israeli desert at fourteen hundred feet below sea level, is a region of extreme heat and dryness. From En Gedi one finds an enticing view of the Dead Sea, which looks decidedly refreshing to a hot, thirsty traveler. Unfortunately, looks are deceiving, as the Dead Sea water is a deadly concoction of 32 percent salts with a high concentration of minerals such as magnesium, calcium, bromide, and potassium—anything but refreshing drinking water.

In much the same way, the world entices our souls, appearing refreshing and pleasing to the eye—until, that is, we partake of its pleasures. But to fill our spiritual thirst with anything other than Jesus is to attempt a superficial solution for a deep spiritual need.

Psalm 42:1-2 reminds us of David as he fled from Saul through the rough terrain and climate of En Gedi.

The passage says, "As the deer pants for the water brooks, so pants my soul for You, O God. My soul thirsts for God, for the living God." Here the word "thirsts" carries the idea of intense craving, longing, yearning, or lusting and describes a spiritual condition. What a beautiful picture of God being likened to water that satisfies our physical thirst.

We all thirst in several ways:

1. We thirst physically—for water. When we lack water, our bodies become dehydrated. Physical thirst creates in us an intense craving for water, and there is no mistaking what will satisfy that thirst. Water is key in regulating body temperature, among other functions, and without water we will die.

2. We thirst emotionally—for love, affection, and acceptance. This world promises to fill the longing in our hearts for love, affection, and acceptance, but its promises always fall short of any lasting satisfaction. Many times people turn to other people or to things to fulfill their emotional thirsts, but as long as the roots of their problems remain, so do their thirsts. The only true source of satisfaction is the love, comfort, and acceptance of God.

3. We thirst spiritually—for worship. Everyone worships something; indeed, we were created for that reason. If we don't have a relationship with Jesus, we will try to fill our *spiritual* thirst for worship with the wrong *physical* things. In the past people worshiped physical idols made of stone and metal. People still worship idols today, but they take on different forms. For example, money and material possessions

can easily become idols if we allow them to take the place of God in our lives. Instead of putting God first, we serve money and things—they become our primary goals, and in turn, they end up controlling us. Jesus warned of this in Matthew 6:24: "No one can serve two masters; you cannot serve both God and money" (NIV).

*It's a safe thing to trust Him to fulfill the desires which He creates.*

**Amy Carmichael**

People turn to many things in an attempt to quench their spiritual thirsts. Pleasure, sex, obsession with youth, entertainment, social prestige, popularity, body image, one's children or spouse, power, career, possessions, even loved ones who have passed away can become master passions. Most of these things are not evil in and of themselves, but they can become sinful if we allow them to rule our lives. Left unchecked, the desire for the things we think will quench our thirst can lead to jealousy, bitterness, and every evil thing (see Heb. 12:15; James 3:14–16). According to God's Word, we have been born with a spiritual void in our hearts that only Jesus can sufficiently fill (see Eccles. 3:11; Rom. 8:20–21).

Maybe you have been running frantically from place to place, searching for something that will bring satisfaction to your spiritual thirst that only God can satisfy. Maybe you have tried everything to bring peace and joy, forgiveness, and a sense of belonging into your life. Jesus said, "Whoever drinks of this [physical] water will thirst again" (John 4:13). But Jesus, the living water, will come into your heart and quench your thirsts. All you have to do is believe in Him and ask!

Being honest and open with God is vital in dealing with our root issues. He already knows everything about us, but He is waiting for us to turn to Him for healing. We were not created for this world but for eternity with God. Our problems begin when we strive to fill our lives with the temporal things of this world, when the only thing that can truly satisfy is Jesus.

*Only one life, 'twill soon be past, only what's done for Christ will last.*

**C. T. Studd**

I was raised in a moral home with a good family, although we were not involved in a church or taught the Word of God. Being the youngest of three children, I was given a lot of freedom. I had almost anything I wanted materially speaking, but I soon found that freedom and material goods coupled with a spiritual vacuum was a recipe for failure. I wasted a lot of time pursuing what I thought would make me happy, but as I tried to satisfy my spiritual thirst with temporal things, I was left more empty than ever before.

It wasn't until I surrendered my life to Jesus Christ and allowed Him to fill me with His Spirit that I understood the deep satisfaction of a quenched soul. God not only created me, but He also sustains and *satisfies* the longings in my heart.

This week as Jesus calls you to come to Him, it is important to understand that *His calling is not dependent upon who you are, what you have done, or even what has been done to you. Rather, He calls you solely because He has created you and loves you with an everlasting, unconditional love.* God knows everything about you, your past, and your current situation. He knows how you feel, and He knows you have wounds, but as you allow Him to touch and transform you, He will heal your wounds and fill the void in your heart.

1. List the things that you have used in the past to quench your emotional or spiritual thirst.

2. Perhaps you are presently using things to quench your emotional or spiritual thirst. Pray that the Lord would reveal these things as His Spirit speaks to your heart and help you commit them all to Him. As you confess these things to God and ask Him to fill you with His Spirit, your spirit will be refreshed.

*Repent therefore and be converted, that your sins may be blotted out, so that times of refreshing may come from the presence of the Lord.*

**Acts 3:19**

## DAY 2: SPIRITUAL THIRST

We thirst spiritually because we have been created to be satisfied by God alone, both in this present life and for all eternity. The things of this world constantly work to draw us away, causing us to live for the pleasures of this life while avoiding our spiritual need. The good news is that Jesus is calling us to Himself so that He can satisfy the longings in our souls. The bad news is that without accepting the finished work of Jesus on the cross, we will be eternally separated from God (see Isa. 59:1–2). Jesus said in John 14:6, "I am the way, the truth, and the life. No one comes to the Father except through Me."

The reality of eternal life with Jesus in heaven and eternal life without Jesus in hell is found in Luke 16:19–31. In these scriptures we see two men: one extremely rich and the other, Lazarus, extremely poor. The rich man, who lived in luxury with all his temporal needs fulfilled, was confident of his own position in life and callous to the plight of Lazarus, showing him no love, sympathy, or compassion. Lazarus, on the other hand, having desperate physical needs, was reduced to lying outside the gate of this rich man's house, hoping to eat what would fall from his table. Eventually both died. Lazarus went to heaven to be eternally present with God, and the rich man went to hell, eternally separated from God.

In this story Jesus teaches that both heaven and hell are real, literal places. The Bible is clear that every person who has ever lived will spend eternity in one or the other. Like the rich man, multitudes today are complacent when it comes to their need for God because they are satisfied with earthly things.

None of us knows when we will take our last breath, but when that day and moment come, our eternal fate will be sealed. We will have no second chances. The transition to our eternal state takes place the moment we die (see Luke 23:43). When believers die, they are immediately in conscious fellowship with the Father and the joys of heaven, with every thirst completely satisfied for eternity (see 2 Cor. 5:8; Phil. 1:23). When unbelievers die, they are immediately in conscious pain and suffering, with unquenchable thirst and the torments of hell for eternity (see Matt. 25:41; Jude 1:7). The rich man was eternally separated from God, and he had no hope of ever being comforted in his pain, suffering, or sorrow.

Many today believe a type of "prosperity gospel," as did the rich man who wrongly believed that his material riches were evidence of God's love and blessing. The rich man mistakenly thought that God had cursed the poor and destitute. This is not what Scripture teaches. In fact, the apostle James exhorts us, "You have lived on earth in luxury and self-indulgence. You have fattened yourselves in the day of slaughter" (James 5:5, NIV). Riches are not necessarily evidence of God's approval; in reality, they have the power to separate a person from God. Mark 4:19 says that "the cares of this world, the deceitfulness of riches, and the desires for other things entering in choke the word, and it becomes unfruitful."

1. Read Isaiah 55:6–7, and record it below word for word.

A. Based on this scripture, when should you seek God?

B. What is God willing to do for a repentant heart?

C. How does this truth affect your life?

Scripture helps us understand that God's children, like Lazarus, can suffer while on this earth. Suffering is actually *promised* to us in Scripture; it is one of the most tragic consequences of living in a sinful, fallen world.

2. Record what Jesus said in John 16:33. While we are *promised* tribulation, what does Jesus *offer* us?

God not only created us, but He sustains our lives every day. Acts 17:28 tells us that it is "in Him we live and move and have our being." He has a purpose for our lives, but we will only realize that purpose as we come to Him, desiring to know Him more. When we do, He will offer us a peace that passes understanding in our situations (see Phil. 4:7).

God loves us so much that He allows us to choose our eternal destination. If we choose to live apart from God during our time on earth, He will allow us to live apart from Him for eternity as well. But if we choose to turn to Him and trust Him to fulfill our spiritual thirst, He promises that we will be with Him in paradise for eternity.

The day each of us is faced with death, only one thing will matter—our relationship with Jesus Christ—because eternal life is found in none other than Him. Today is the day to choose whom we will serve—whom we will allow to satisfy our thirsty soul. Our choice will have eternal consequences.

3. Write out 1 John 5:11–12 and then answer the following questions.

A. Based on this passage, who has given us eternal life?

B. Where is this life found?

C. Who has eternal life?

D. Who does not have eternal life?

4. Do you have the same desire that David expressed in Psalm 42:1?

*To promise heaven and not warn of hell, to offer forgiveness without repentance, to preach the gospel without the cross is a false message giving false hope.*

**Greg Laurie**

If you have not surrendered your life to Jesus, you can do so right now. Be transparent with God through prayer as you acknowledge the truth about yourself, understand your need for a Savior, and believe that Jesus alone can save you from your sins. Repent, and ask Him to forgive you of anything that is not pleasing to Him.

Eternal life is a free gift, and it can be yours today if you simply believe in your heart that Jesus is Lord, that God raised Him from the dead, and that He paid the price for your sins on the cross. If you accept the finished work of Jesus on the cross and allow Him into your life to do the work He desires to do—to touch and transform your life for His glory—you can be certain of eternal life with Him.

Perhaps you have accepted Jesus as your personal Savior but have not been pursuing Him as the means to quench your thirst on a daily basis. He is calling—will you respond?

5. If you are doing this study with a leader, talk to him or her about your decision and what it means to you. You can also talk with a pastor, church leader, or mature Christian friend. Confirm your decision by writing words of thanksgiving to Jesus below.

*By grace you have been saved through faith, and that not of yourselves; it is the gift of God, not of works, lest anyone should boast. For we are His workmanship, created in Christ Jesus for good works, which God prepared beforehand that we should walk in them.*

**Ephesians 2:8–10**

## DAY 3: THE SAMARITAN WOMAN AND A RELIGIOUS LEADER

Today, in one sitting, prayerfully read John 3:1–21 and 4:1–42. The first passage records Jesus' meeting with Nicodemus and the second His encouter with a Samaritan woman. As you read, keep the following questions in mind:

What do I learn about

- God/Jesus/the Holy Spirit?

- The lies of Satan?

- My situation?

- Myself/my beliefs?

- The truth of God's Word?

Is there

- A command or example in the passage for me to follow?

- A false identity I need to confess?

- A lie that needs replacing with God's truth?

- Something I need to repent of?

- A sin or judgment I need to avoid?

- Something I need to surrender and trust God with?

Write your thoughts below.

Respond to the Lord by writing a prayer.

God graciously meets us right where we are, no matter our position or situation in life, and Jesus met the Samaritan woman according to her personal need. In the preceding chapter of John's Gospel, however, Jesus expresses God's grace toward Nicodemus, a proud Pharisee and prominent member of the Jewish Sanhedrin, in a very different way.

1. Having read the story of Nicodemus in John 3:1–21, record your impressions.

2. Read James 4:6 and 1 Peter 5:5, and paraphrase how God deals with pride.

*Pride goes before destruction, and a haughty spirit before a fall.*
**Proverbs 16:18**

While we see similarities in the conversations between Jesus and Nicodemus and the Samaritan woman, we also see a contrast in the way Jesus unveiled His grace to each one. Both realized that they were under God's law but could not keep it because they were lawbreakers by nature. But Nicodemus needed to see himself as a sinner in order to understand his need for grace, while the Samaritan woman already knew she was a sinner and needed to see herself as a person of worth and value. Both equally needed God's grace! Whether we are like Nicodemus or the Samaritan woman, when we understand that we can never measure up to God's law, His grace becomes precious to us.

3. What new truth did you discover in these two stories?

4. Which person best describes your life—Nicodemus or the Samaritan woman? Give reasons for your answer.

5. Look up and read Romans 5:8. When did Christ die for you?

> *God must do everything for us. Our part is to yield and trust.*
>
> **A. W. Tozer**

6. Look up and read John 3:3–6. What does it mean to be born again?

> *God so loved the world that He gave His only begotten Son, that whoever believes in Him should not perish but have everlasting life. For God did not send His Son into the world to condemn the world, but that the world through Him might be saved.*
>
> **John 3:16–17**

## DAY 4: THE SOURCE OF LIVING WATER

Yesterday we read about Jesus' conversation with a Samaritan woman. Samaritans were a race of people that the Jews utterly despised as pagans. The Samaritan woman was an outcast with her own people as well, which was probably why she came alone in the heat of the day to draw water from the community well. During biblical times drawing water at the well was the social highlight of a woman's day, but this woman was ostracized, marked as an immoral woman, since she was unmarried and in her fifth relationship. Her life was a perfect picture of trying to satisfy spiritual and emotional thirst with things that cannot satisfy.

The story of the Samaritan woman teaches us that God finds us worthy of His love in spite of our bankrupt lives. Even though God knows our deficiencies, He values us enough to actively seek us and invite us into a relationship with Him. Surely this Samaritan woman who was rejected by her own people—alone, abandoned, and feeling worthless—could appreciate the value of being sought after and cared for when no one, not even she, could see anything of value in her. Such a wonderful picture of God's grace!

Jesus is omniscient, meaning that He knows all things, even the things we are ashamed of, the things we don't want to admit, the things we try to hide. When we come face to face with God and realize that He knows all these things yet still desires a relationship with us, it will cause an openness in us and a desire to repent—a desire to turn from our lives without Him and accept His invitation with open arms. "There is no creature hidden from His sight, but all things are naked and open to the eyes of Him to whom we must give account" (Heb. 4:13).

1. According to John 4:28–29, what resulted from the Samaritan woman's encounter with Jesus?

2. The Samaritan woman had come to the well for physical water and instead found living water. As

her spiritual thirst was quenched, her life was so transformed that she couldn't help but tell others about Jesus, inviting them to come and see Him for themselves. Jesus used physical water as a metaphor of the spiritual water that He alone can provide through His Holy Spirit. What did Jesus say to this woman in John 4:13–14?

*Satan's plan for your life promises pleasure but delivers pain as he leads you down the path of death and destruction. Jesus' plan promises temporal pain but delivers pleasure as He leads you on the upward path of eternal life.*

3. Jesus' encounter with this outcast Samaritan woman shows that everyone, regardless of upbringing, social status, gender, education, or popularity, is equally valuable to God. In what way does Peter describe a repentant sinner who comes to Jesus in 1 Peter 2:9–10?

*Only fear the LORD, and serve Him in truth with all your heart; for consider what great things He has done for you.*

**1 Samuel 12:24**

4. Write out Psalm 63:1–5 here, and make it your prayer.

*The hour is coming, and now is, when the true worshipers will worship the Father in spirit and truth; for the Father is seeking such to worship Him. God is Spirit, and those who worship Him must worship in spirit and truth.*

**John 4:23–24**

## DAY 5: THE NAMES OF GOD

As we saw in week 1, it's not enough to know *about* someone if we want to have deep relationship with that individual—we must really *know* the person. It's the same with God—if we want to have a growing relationship with Him, we must get to know Him. One way of doing this is to learn His names, which He has revealed to us in the Scripture, as His names reveal to us His character and attributes.

Every name of God reveals to us something specific about Him. Today we will look at three names of God, each one showing us that He is personal, powerful, and totally in control. These attributes make clear that God is fully able to sustain and satisfy us, completely quenching our spiritual thirst.

### ELOHIM—GOD OUR CREATOR

*Elohim* is the first name for God mentioned in the Scripture, and we find it in the opening verse of Scripture: "In the beginning God [*Elohim*] created the heavens and the earth" (Gen. 1:1). God the Creator made each of us with a purpose, and He is the One who both created and satisfies our every hunger and thirst.

The Hebrew words for "God" are *El* (singular), *El-o* (dual), and *El-o-him* (plural). The use of the word *Elohim* does not indicate many gods; rather it is used to emphasize the majesty and plurality of the one true God. We see this reference to the triune God in 1 John 5:7: "There are three that bear witness in heaven: the Father, the Word [Jesus], and the Holy Spirit; and these three are one." The use of *Elohim* in Genesis 1:1 reveals to us that all three persons of the Godhead—God the Father, God the Son, and God the Holy Spirit—were present at creation.

This plurality of God is also mentioned in John 1:1–4, which gives us specific insight into Jesus, the second person of the Trinity: "In the beginning was the Word, and the Word was with God, and the Word was God. He [Jesus] was in the beginning with God. All things were made through Him, and without Him nothing was made that was made. In Him was life, and the life was the light of men."

1. Read John 1:14, and answer the questions below.
   A. Who is the Word?


   B. I never tire of reading Psalm 119, which speaks of the Scriptures and the benefits of studying God's Word. All but three verses in this chapter have some reference to the Word of God. Read Psalm 119:1–8, and replace the phrases concerning God's law, statutes, commandments, precepts, testimonies, and other terms that refer to the Word of God with the name "Jesus." (If you want to dig deeper, you can do this with the entire psalm—it is a powerful exercise showing the many benefits by which Jesus, the Word, meets our needs and quenches our thirst.) Then respond to Jesus by writing a prayer of thanksgiving for all the benefits He gives us as we learn more about Him through His Word.

2. Who does Jesus claim to be, according to Revelation 1:8?

These verses we have just read, among others, show that *Elohim*, the triune God, was fully present at and active in creation. They further show that Jesus is not a created being but that *He is God*, the Creator.

3. In Psalm 139:13–17 below, underline what it says about Jesus. Then go over the passage again, this time circling what it says about you.

> You formed my inward parts; You covered me in my mother's womb. I will praise You, for I am fearfully and wonderfully made; marvelous are Your works, and that my soul knows very well. My frame was not hidden from You, when I was made in secret, and skillfully wrought in the lowest parts of the earth. Your eyes saw my substance, being yet unformed. And in Your book they all were written, the days fashioned for me, when as yet there were none of them.
>
> How precious also are Your thoughts to me, O God! How great is the sum of them!

4. Look up the promise associated with *Elohim* in Isaiah 41:10, and record what blesses you most.

5. Consider the fact that God not only created you but also thinks about you and wants to satisfy your deepest longings because of His unending, unparalleled love for you. Respond by writing a prayer of thanksgiving to Him.

His name is *Elohim*—His name is Jesus!

## EL ELYON—GOD MOST HIGH

The name *El Elyon* emphasizes God's transcendence; He is God Most High above every realm of life and over every aspect of the universe. In other words, He is Almighty God, the exalted One, and because of this, He has the power to sustain all life and satisfy our every longing.

The name *El Elyon* is first found in Genesis 14:18 in relation to Melchizedek, the king of Salem. God is further revealed as *El Elyon* in Daniel's account of Nebuchadnezzar, an arrogant Babylonian king. Nebuchadnezzar was so prideful in his own accomplishments that God humbled him to the lowest point possible, making him crawl around in the fields eating grass like an animal. It wasn't until God humbled him that he finally acknowledged God as Most High and returned to a sound mind.

1. Read the following passage from Daniel 4:34–37, underlining Nebuchadnezzar's realization about God.

   > At the end of the time I, Nebuchadnezzar, lifted my eyes to heaven, and my understanding returned to me; and I blessed the Most High and praised and honored Him who lives forever: For His dominion is an everlasting dominion, and His kingdom is from generation to generation. All the inhabitants of the earth are reputed as nothing; He does according to His will in the army of heaven and

among the inhabitants of the earth. No one can restrain His hand or say to Him, "What have You done?" At the same time my reason returned to me, and for the glory of my kingdom, my honor and splendor returned to me. My counselors and nobles resorted to me, I was restored to my kingdom, and excellent majesty was added to me. Now I, Nebuchadnezzar, praise and extol and honor the King of heaven, all of whose works are truth, and His ways justice. And those who walk in pride He is able to put down.

*The knowledge of the Holy One is understanding.*

**Proverbs 9:10**

2. Sometimes, like Nebuchadnezzar, we lose sight of the fact that God is big. Record what 2 Samuel 7:22 says about God.

3. *El Elyon* means that He is elevated as the supreme God; there is no God higher than Him. Read Acts 7:47–50, and write out Stephen's words from verses 48–50 about *El Elyon*.

4. When we cry out to *El Elyon*—God Most High—what can we be assured of, according to Psalm 57:2–3?

5. Look up the promise associated with *El Elyon* in the following verses, and record what blesses you most.

Psalm 91:1–2:

Psalm 91:9–11:

*I know the thoughts that I think toward you, says the LORD, thoughts of peace and not of evil, to give you a future and a hope. Then you will call upon Me and go and pray to Me, and I will listen to you. And you will seek Me and find Me, when you search for Me with all your heart. I will be found by you, says the LORD, and I will bring you back from your captivity.*

**Jeremiah 29:11–14**

6. Jesus is *El Elyon*—He is God over all things; He is Lord. Respond to Him for loving you with an everlasting, satisfying love by writing out a prayer to Him.

*I will praise the LORD according to His righteousness, and will sing praise to the name of the LORD Most High.*

**Psalm 7:17**

His name is *El Elyon*—His name is Jesus!

## EL SHADDAI—GOD ALMIGHTY, GATEKEEPER

God is not only the Creator and God Most High, but He is also the almighty God who maintains His covenant with His people. Until the time of Moses, *El Shaddai* was considered to be the covenant name of God, meaning that *El Shaddai* would keep His promises. If God said it, you could count on it. It's still true today. God's promises are not conditional but are based upon the unchanging, unwavering character of an immutable God: "If we are faithless, He remains faithful; He cannot deny Himself" (2 Tim. 2:13).

The book of Genesis records this name in the account of Abram (Abraham) and Sarai (Sarah). The story begins in Genesis 15:5–6, where the Lord, the self-existent, eternal God, appeared to Abram, saying, "Look now toward heaven, and count the stars if you are able to number them. . . . So shall your descendants be." Abraham believed God, and the Lord "accounted it to him for righteousness."

But while Abram and Sarai liked the idea of God's promise, they grew impatient as time passed and Sarai did not give birth to any children. Because they failed to realize that God is Almighty, able to do the impossible, Sarai advised Abram to take her handmaiden Hagar and have relations with her (an acceptable practice in those days) in order to see the promise of God come to pass. In other words, instead of patiently waiting upon the Lord, they reacted in the flesh and tried to help God fulfill His promise by taking matters into their own hands. This ended up in disaster. Sarai became jealous of Hagar, and she mistreated her servant harshly.

*Those who live according to the flesh set their minds on the things of the flesh, but those who live according to the Spirit, the things of the Spirit. . . . So then, those who are in the flesh cannot please God.*

*But you are not in the flesh but in the Spirit, if indeed the Spirit of God dwells [abides] in you.*

**Romans 8:5, 8–9**

Although they acted according to the flesh, God showed His great mercy and patience for Abram and Sarai by giving them another chance to trust Him with their lives and futures. Genesis 17:1–4 tells us that when Abram was ninety-nine years old, the Lord appeared to him again and said,

> "I am Almighty God [*El Shaddai*]; walk before Me and be blameless. And I will make My covenant between Me and you, and will multiply you exceedingly." Then Abram fell on his face, and God talked with him, saying: "As for Me, behold, My covenant is with you, and you shall be a father of many nations."

God is always faithful to His promises and never needs our help to fulfill them, because He is *El Shaddai*, the almighty God. Abram and Sarai eventually realized that they could trust God and take Him at His word. In fact, both Abraham and Sarah are listed in Hebrews 11 along with others who are recognized for their faith, not their unbelief. They finally chose to wait and abide in God's promise, believing that He is sufficient and that nothing is too hard for Him. "Is anything too hard for the LORD? At the appointed time I will return to you, according to the time of life, and Sarah shall have a son" (Gen. 18:14).

The name *El Shaddai*, which is mentioned forty-eight times in the Old Testament, has a secondary meaning: "gatekeeper." Although this is not often taught, I learned it from my Israeli guide in Israel, as he and another man I met most emphatically assured me that *El Shaddai* is understood to be the "gatekeeper." What does this mean?

In John 10:7–9 Jesus tells us, "Most assuredly, I say to you, I am the door of the sheep. All who ever came before Me are thieves and robbers, but the sheep did not hear them. I am the door. If anyone enters by Me, he will be saved, and will go in and out and find pasture." Jesus is *El Shaddai*, our gatekeeper, meaning that He is in complete control of our circumstances. Nothing can come in or out of our lives unless it passes through Him first. Furthermore, He will draw us into a deeper relationship with Him through everything He allows to touch our lives.

When you are tempted to rely upon your own strength, understanding, or intellect, or when you grow impatient because things are not turning out how you expect, acknowledge that God is your *El Shaddai*. Only as you abide in Him and His Word will you experience true rest, because He alone is sufficient to quench our spiritual thirst. Jesus is the almighty gatekeeper—He is *El Shaddai*!

1. Look up the promise associated with *El Shaddai* in Proverbs 18:10, and record what blesses you most.

*We have such trust through Christ toward God. Not that we are sufficient of ourselves to think of anything as being from ourselves, but our sufficiency is from God, who also made us sufficient as ministers of the new covenant, not of the letter but of the Spirit; for the letter kills, but the Spirit gives life.*

**2 Corinthians 3:4–6**

His name is *El Shaddai*—His name is Jesus!

### NAMES OF GOD REVIEW

1. Jesus is *Elohim*, your Creator. How does knowing that He created you and has given your life purpose impact your life today?

2. Jesus is *El Elyon*, God Most High. What did you learn about *El Elyon* that you did not realize before this study?

3. Jesus is *El Shaddai*; He is God Almighty who keeps His promises, and He is your gatekeeper. God is faithful to His covenant and faithful to sufficiently satisfy your soul as He watches over you. Is there a promise of God that you cannot fathom being worked out in your life? If so, why do you see it as being impossible?

*The LORD will guide you continually, and satisfy your soul in drought, and strengthen your bones; you shall be like a watered garden, and like a spring of water, whose waters do not fail.*

**Isaiah 58:11**

4. Which biblical example were you most able to relate to this week—the rich man, Lazarus, the Samaritan woman, Nicodemus, Nebuchadnezzar, Abram, or Sarai? Explain.

*O God, I have tasted Thy goodness, and it has both satisfied me and made me thirsty for more. I am painfully conscious of my need for further grace. I am ashamed of my lack of desire. O God, the Triune God, I want to want Thee; I long to be filled with longing; I thirst to be made more thirsty still. Show me Thy glory, I pray Thee, so that I may know Thee indeed. Begin in mercy a new work of love within me. Say to my soul, "Rise up my love, my fair one, and come away." Then give me grace to rise and follow Thee up from this misty lowland where I have wandered so long.*

**A. W. Tozer**

5. How does knowing Jesus as *Elohim*, *El Elyon*, and *El Shaddai* help you today in your situation?

His name is *Elohim*—God our Creator.

His name is *El Elyon*—God Most High.

His name is *El Shaddai*—God Almighty, our gatekeeper.

His name is Jesus!

# Week 3

## TOUCHED AND TRANSFORMED BY HIS LOVE

*I have declared to them Your name, and will declare it, that the love with which You loved Me may be in them, and I in them.*

John 17:26

### DAY 1: GOD IS LOVE

Perhaps you are seeking healing from a life-changing event and desperately need to experience God's love and forgiveness. I can't think of more beautiful words than those found in Jeremiah 31:3: "I have loved you with an everlasting love; therefore with loving-kindness I have drawn you." It is easy for us to forget who God is, especially when things don't seem to line up with what we think about Him or when we are overwhelmed with the guilt of our sin, but during difficult times we need to fall back on what we know to be true. The Word of God is truth, and it tells us that God's love for us is real.

Unfortunately, people often have preconceived ideas about God, and many believe that God is just waiting for them to mess up so He can punish them. Of course, this viewpoint could not be further from the truth. Jesus took the punishment, pain, beatings, and persecution on my behalf, bearing my sins Himself. In John 15:13 Jesus tells us, "Greater love has no one than this, than to lay down one's life for his friends." This is a love we can never fully comprehend, because only God can love like this.

While we have only one word for "love" in the English language, the Greek has four. The first three are *eros*, carrying the idea of sexual love, *phileo*, referring to friendly love, and *storgae*, meaning the love a parent has for a child. These three words all have a self-centered motivation behind them. In other words, I *eros* you if I am physically attracted to you; I *phileo* you if you are my friend; and I *storgae* you if you are my child.

The fourth word for love is *agape*, and this one carries the idea of unconditional love—the kind of love God has for His children. Only God is capable of giving this kind of love; He is the source of *agape*, and He desires us to pour it out into our lives so that we might "know the love of Christ which passes knowledge; that [we] might be filled with all the fullness of God" (Eph. 3:19).

In the book of Hosea, we read an almost unbelievable story of God commanding one of His prophets to marry a prostitute. In this story the prophet Hosea represents Jesus as God's obedient and faithful servant. Gomer, the prostitute, is a picture of Israel, which we as believers are now grafted into (see Rom. 11:16–24).

Hosea did as God commanded him, choosing Gomer to be his wife. For reasons we are not told, Gomer soon left Hosea and returned to her old life of prostitution. Heartbroken, Hosea raised their children as a single father. After a period of time, God told Hosea to search for Gomer and receive her again. Hosea found his prostitute wife and brought her back home, where he continued to love her and tend to her needs as though she had never left.

God uses this story to illustrate the unconditional, unfailing *agape* love He has for His people. Like Gomer, God's people can choose to turn their backs on the Lord, proving themselves unfaithful to their commitment to Him. Those who are indifferent to God's love willfully live their lives with no thought of Him, refusing to honor Him with their lives. Despite these facts, our merciful and loving God calls us back to Him with a wonderful promise, saying, "I will heal their backsliding, I will love them freely" (Hos. 14:4).

This kind of love and forgiveness is not deserved but is purely by God's grace. God's love extends beyond the limits of our sinful humanity, and despite our wanderings, failings, and unfaithfulness, He longs to restore us to right relationship with Him. God doesn't command us to be perfect; He just invites us to respond to His love. "I have blotted out, like a thick cloud, your transgressions, and like a cloud, your sins. Return to Me, for I have redeemed you" (Isa. 44:22).

1. Just as Hosea received a prostitute as his wife and committed to love her, so too Christ has loved you and accepted you as His bride. Read Ephesians 2:4–7, and record how it relates to your life.

2. When Jesus came in the form of man (see John 1:14), He came not to condemn you but to save you. He knows you and loves you personally. He would have died for you even if you had been the only one in need of saving. He knows the worst about you and yet loves you more than anyone else does. Fill in the blank in John 3:16 below, personalizing it so that it says to you, "I am the one He came to die for."

God so loved _____
that He gave His only begotten Son, that *whoever* believes in Him should not perish but have everlasting life.

3. The biggest strongholds in our lives stem from not understanding God's love for us. How does John 15:13–15 speak to your heart about God's love?

When we understand God's everlasting, unlimited, sacrificial love, we realize that everything He does is for our eternal benefit. Instead of wanting to hit us over the head, God is calling us unto Himself so that He can pour out His love on us.

4. Read and comment on 1 John 4:9–10.

    A. What has God revealed about His love for you today?

    B. There is no doubt that God loves you with an unconditional love. The question is, do you love God? Explain.

5. What evidence in your life shows that you have accepted the love God expresses in 2 John 6?

*As the Father loved Me, I also have loved you; abide in My love.*

**John 15:9**

6. What does John 14:15 tell us Jesus says?

## DAY 2: THE FALL OF MAN AND THE LOVE OF GOD

As we look more fully into God's love for sinful people, prayerfully read Genesis 3, which tells the story of Adam and Eve's fall into sin and God's response to them.

God created mankind for perfect, unhindered fellowship with Himself. However, when sin entered the garden through the serpent (see Ezek. 28:13–17), Eve was deceived, and she then convinced Adam to partake of the only forbidden thing in the garden: the tree of the knowledge of good and evil. Satan purposely sought to deceive the woman rather than the man; she was more vulnerable to attack, since she had not received the command not to eat of the tree directly from God, as Adam had (see Gen. 2:16). This shows the importance of personally hearing from God and testing His voice according to the Bible.

*The Lord God took the man and put him in the garden of Eden to tend and keep it. And the Lord God commanded the man, saying, "Of every tree of the garden you may freely eat; but of the tree of the knowledge of good and evil you shall not eat, for in the day that you eat of it you shall surely die."*

**Genesis 2:15–17**

From the beginning Satan has tried to undermine God's Word of truth. The most effective way for the enemy to deceive us is by getting us to question God's Word. Satan effectively drew Eve into a discussion and planted the seed of doubt about God's word to her and Adam, and he exposed her incomplete understanding of the love of

God. When our roots are weak, as we saw in week 1, we can easily be deceived and fall away from the truth. This is why we are called to never give place to the devil (see Eph. 4:27) and to be rooted and grounded in the love of God (see Eph. 3:17).

While Eve was deceived, Adam sinned with his eyes wide open, in open rebellion against God. Nonetheless, both sinned, and this sin broke their unhindered fellowship with God. Immediately they realized they were naked and tried to cover their shame with fig leaves. They also made excuses for their sin (see Gen. 3:9–13). This attempt to shift blame is completely consistent with our human sinful nature. Making excuses for our sin will never make things right with a holy God, and working to cover our sin will never be sufficient to take away our guilt and shame.

In order for Adam and Eve to be properly clothed figuratively, a sacrifice had to be made—an animal had to die. Hebrews 9:22 tells us that "without shedding of blood there is no remission." As God clothed Adam and Eve with the skins of animals, He provided a literal covering for them through a sacrifice. This act of mercy was symbolic of how our loving God would later provide the perfect sacrifice through Jesus, who would not only cover our sin but take away the sin of the world (see John 1:29).

Just like Adam and Eve, we don't get to choose what we use to cover our sin; our only choice is to receive God's covering, or propitiation. Greek-American Bible scholar Spiros Zodhiates defines propitiation this way:

The lid or covering of the ark of the covenant made of pure gold, on and before which the high priest was to sprinkle the blood of the expiatory [that which makes amends or reparations for] sacrifices on the Day of Atonement [the one day a year that sacrifices and offerings were made on behalf of the sins of the people], [is] where the Lord promised to meet His people (Ex. 25:7, 22; Lev. 16:2, 14, 15). Paul, by applying this name to Christ in Rom. 3:25, assures us that Christ was the true mercy seat, the reality typified by the cover on the ark of the covenant (Heb. 9:5). Therefore, it means a place of conciliation, of expiation, what the ancients called . . . altar or place of sacrifice. Jesus Christ is designated . . . not only as the place where the sinner deposits his sin, but He Himself is the means of expiation. He is not like the high priest of the OT whose expiation of the people was accomplished through the blood of something other than himself (Heb. 9:25).[1]

The mercy seat refers to Jesus Christ and is the equivalent to the throne of grace. The idea is that God Himself, out of His great love for sinners, provided the way by which His wrath against us might be averted. Jesus shed His blood and became the way to the Father for sinners.

*Above all things have fervent love for one another, for "love will cover a multitude of sins."*

**1 Peter 4:8**

This is the *agape* love of God, a love like no other!

It is foolish for us to try to cover our nakedness, or sin. We need to determine to put on Jesus Himself as our covering garment (see Gal. 3:27). The exhortation from

Jesus in Revelation 16:15 is for us: "Behold, I am coming as a thief. Blessed is he who watches, and keeps his garments, lest he walk naked and they see his shame."

Because Adam and Eve sinned, they would suffer consequences, but these consequences did not change God's love. Ultimately, sin brought death to all, but because of His great love, Jesus tasted death for everyone that we might be saved (see Heb. 2:9).

1. Look up Romans 3:23–26, and comment on what it says about God's love for you (even though the word "love" is not mentioned).

2. How did Jesus show the depth of His love for you, according to 1 Peter 2:24–25?

3. What did God do on your behalf, according to Ephesians 2:13?

4. Stop and think about the depths of God's love for you. Respond to the Lord by writing a prayer below thanking Him for His unfailing, everlasting love.

### DAY 3: THE SIN OF DAVID

Anointed by God as a young shepherd boy tending his father's sheep, David became king of Israel when he was thirty-seven years old. God Himself calls David a man after His own heart (see Acts 13:22) because of David's great love for his Lord. Throughout David's life God's loving hand was upon him. We see this in 2 Samuel 8:6, which tells us that "the LORD preserved David wherever he went." God brought peace to the empire and prosperity to the people through David's reign. However, it was when things were going really well that David's troubles began.

Spend time today prayerfully reading 2 Samuel 11–12:25; read with purpose, asking the following:

What do I learn about

- God/Jesus/the Holy Spirit?

- The lies of Satan?

- My situation?

- Myself/my beliefs?

- The truth of God's Word?

Is there

- A command or example in the passage for me to follow?

- A false identity I need to confess?

- A lie that needs replacing with God's truth?

- Something I need to repent of?

- A sin or judgment I need to avoid?

- Something I need to surrender and trust God with?

Write your findings below.

Respond to God by writing a prayer.

The spring of each year was when kings went to war, but according to 2 Samuel 11, this particular spring David decided to stay in Jerusalem and let his military personnel fight his battles for him. We are not told why he stayed behind, but this one act of isolation left David vulnerable to the desires of his flesh. As David walked alone one evening on the roof of his house, he saw a beautiful woman bathing and sent someone to find out who she was. David learned that she was Bathsheba, the wife of Uriah the Hittite, one of his own warriors. He foolishly sent for her in a moment of lustful desire and slept with her. Afterward she returned to her house.

David's adulterous affair was not without consequences. Second Samuel 11:5 states that "the woman conceived; so she sent and told David, and said, 'I am with child.'" David immediately devised a plan to cover his sin by sending for her husband, Uriah. David believed that having Uriah home for a few days with his wife would provide a legitimate explanation for Bathsheba becoming pregnant. But it didn't work out that way. As we saw with Adam and Eve, our devices for covering up our sin are never successful in God's sight. In fact, Numbers 32:23 promises, "Be sure your sin will find you out."

Uriah chose to sleep at the door of the king's house with all the servants of his lord, saying he could not enjoy the comforts of home while others were encamped in open fields (see 2 Sam. 11:11). So David sent Uriah back to battle with a letter to Joab, the commander of David's army, instructing Joab to put Uriah at the front of the battle and withdraw the other soldiers, ensuring that Uriah would be killed. David had become so calloused by his sin that he cared only about saving himself at any cost. Joab followed the king's instructions, and Uriah was killed to cover up David's sin. After a period of mourning, Bathsheba became David's wife and eventually gave birth to their son.

1. Read John 8:34. What does Jesus say about the one who commits sin?

A. How is this evident in David's actions?

*A slave does not abide in the house forever, but a son abides forever. Therefore if the Son makes you free, you shall be free indeed.*

**John 8:35–36**

B. How has this practically played out in your life?

2. What warning does Galatians 6:7–8 give?

3. Read Colossians 1:13–14, and answer the following questions regarding what Jesus, because of His great love, has done for you.

A. From what did He deliver you?

B. What have you been conveyed into?

C. Write a response.

*God is able to make all grace abound toward you, that you, always having all sufficiency in all things, may have an abundance for every good work.*

2 Corinthians 9:8

## DAY 4: DAVID'S RESPONSE TO GOD'S LOVE

A year after David's adulterous affair, God was still lovingly and patiently waiting for David to repent of his sin. Because of God's great love for us, He prefers us to come to Him ourselves and repent of our sin so He can forgive us. If we refuse, however, God has no problem stepping in to remind us. God did this with David by sending the prophet Nathan to confront him.

It must not have been easy for Nathan to confront David. He had no guarantee as to how the king would react. David could have killed him, but Nathan exhibited the love of God for David by telling him the truth, being more concerned about obeying the Lord than pleasing the king.

1. Why did Nathan confront David with his sin? See 2 Samuel 12:1 to help you with your answer.

2. What do you learn from the life of David about yourself and about the effect your sin has on others?

3. What are some of the ways people deal with guilt due to unconfessed sin?

*Legalistic remorse says, "I broke God's rules," while real repentance says, "I broke God's heart."*

**Tim Keller**

4. How do you or have you dealt with guilt?

David eventually confessed his sin and repented before his loving God. He did not make excuses; he recognized that what he had done was wrong and ran to God for forgiveness. Repentance goes beyond just being sorry for sin. In Psalm 51 David asked God, "Have mercy upon me . . . according to Your lovingkindness. . . . Wash me thoroughly from my iniquity, and cleanse me from my sin. For I acknowledge my transgressions, and my sin is always before me" (Ps. 51:1–3).

5. Read Matthew 7:3–5. Taking the plank out of your own eye includes looking at the ways your sin has affected others. Answer the questions below on this matter.

   A. Ask God to show you the ways you have negatively affected others.

   B. Who has been affected by your sin?

C. Ask God to forgive you for the ways you have hurt others. Pray right now to receive His forgiveness. What, if anything, can you do to make things right?

6. What leads to repentance, according to Romans 2:4?

7. God is always ready to forgive you. What comfort do you find in 1 John 1:9?

David's soul was plunged into despair until grace delivered and cleansed him—until he received the forgiveness of God. It is through our deepest sins that we bring ourselves the greatest distresses, none more devastating than separation from God (see Isa. 59:1–2).

Yet because of the blood of Jesus, we always have hope of restoration. No matter how deplorable our condition may be, our case *is not hopeless*. The enemy wants us to believe that our sin is too great for us to receive God's forgiveness, but Jesus did not come to condemn us but that through Him we might be set free by His love (see John 3:17). David was a liar, adulterer, and murderer, but as he admitted his sin and cried out to God, God heard his prayer and gave him grace and mercy. This is in accordance with the divine promise found in Hebrews 4:16: "Let us therefore come boldly to the throne of grace, that we may obtain mercy and find grace to help in time of need."

David's life was far from perfect, but his legacy included the bloodline of our Savior, Jesus Christ. God granted David's request, "Create in me a clean heart, O God, and renew a steadfast spirit within me" (Ps. 51:10). God's reaction to David's sin and subsequent confession is consistent with God's words to us throughout the Bible. Psalm 103:11–12 says, "As the heavens are high above the earth, so great is His mercy toward those who fear Him; as far as the east is from the west, so far has He removed our transgressions from us." God tells us in Hebrews 8:12, "I will be merciful to their unrighteousness, and their sins and their lawless deeds I will remember no more." God is willing to forgive, and His forgiveness is complete. He will cleanse our hearts and renew our spirits when we come to Him in honesty and humility, confessing our sin in true repentance. This will restore to us the joy of God's salvation and lead us to freedom from the guilt of our past sin.

In 1 John 1:8–9 the apostle John sums up sin,

repentance, and God's forgiveness this way: "If we say that we have no sin, we deceive ourselves, and the truth is not in us. If we confess our sins, He is faithful and just to forgive us our sins and to cleanse us from all unrighteousness."

8. Read Psalm 51, which shows the depth of David's sorrow and repentance for his sins.

A. What attributes of God do you see in Psalm 51:1 and 7–9 that ensure His forgiveness of your sin?

B. How is forgiveness explained in verse 2?

C. What are the words David uses to indicate his repentance in verses 3–5?

D. Explain what verse 5 says about the state of every person at birth.

E. What does God desire, according to verses 6 and 10–12?

F. Notice in verses 13–15 that David's prayer was not a selfish one. For what purpose did David acknowledge his need for God?

G. What does God *not* desire, according to verse 16?

*The LORD is merciful and gracious, slow to anger, and abounding in mercy.*

**Psalm 103:8**

H. What is acceptable to God, according to verse 17?

Forgiveness means being brought into a right standing before God because of the blood of Jesus, not by any goodness on our part. Many times we hear people say, "I can't forgive myself." Psychology and the world tell us we need to forgive ourselves, but the truth is, we cannot forgive ourselves because forgiveness does not originate with us. Once we understand that all sin is against God, as we see in Psalm 51, we realize that only God can forgive. We must receive His forgiveness to truly be set free from the bondage of our sin and shame.

This is a simple concept but so important for us to grasp. Many Christians believe they have been forgiven but still walk around wearing the grave clothes of self, sin, and bondage to their past. Does that describe you? In spite of any problems we may have, if we've been completely forgiven, we have much to praise God for. "Having been set free from sin, and having become slaves of God, you have your fruit to holiness, and the end, everlasting life. For the wages of sin is death, but the gift of God is eternal life in Christ Jesus our Lord" (Rom. 6:22–23).

It is Jesus who takes away our sins, casting them as far as the east is from the west, but sin's earthly consequences can and will linger. We must be willing to accept whatever consequences our sin brings. God does not cause the consequences, nor does He force righteousness on any man. The world's sin can and will affect us to varying degrees. Regardless of the cause of the consequences, the question we must ask ourselves is, are we willing to trust God? If we know Him to be a loving, merciful God who desires to do us good and not harm, we will trust Him with our lives, including any consequences, knowing that His ways and plans are perfect. "He is the Rock, His work is perfect; for all His ways are justice, a God of truth and without injustice; righteous and upright is He" (Deut. 32:4).

9. Take some time to purposefully and prayerfully read Romans 8:31–39, and record what ministers to you most from this passage.

*Be still, and know that I am God; I will be exalted among the nations, I will be exalted in the earth!*

**Psalm 46:10**

## DAY 5: THE NAMES OF GOD

As we have seen, the names of God reveal the character and nature of God. The more we know His names, the more we will know and trust Him. Today we will look at three names for God that confirm to us His loving and forgiving nature toward sinful men and women.

### Jehovah Tsidqenuw—the Lord Our Righteousness

The Hebrew word *tsidqenuw* (tsid-kay'-noo) means "to make right" or "to be righteous or holy." The name *Jehovah Tsidqenuw* is found in Jeremiah 23:6: "This is His name by which He will be called: THE LORD OUR RIGHTEOUSNESS." Only Jesus is righteous and able to unconditionally love and forgive repentant sinners; He is also the means by which we are not only sanctified but also made righteous, given a right standing before God. Only as we are clothed and covered with the righteousness of Jesus Christ can we stand before a holy God.

1. Look up the promise associated with *Jehovah Tsidqenuw*, the One who clothes us in righteousness, in the following verses.

   Proverbs 10:6–7:



   Proverbs 18:10:

2. Record what blesses you most about the name *Jehovah Tsidqenuw.*

His name is *Jehovah Tsidqenuw*—His name is Jesus!

## EL NASA—GOD WHO FORGIVES

The word *nasa*, meaning "forgive," is first seen in the story of Joseph (see Gen. 50:17) and is found in many scriptures in the Old Testament. The name itself, which means "the God who forgives" or "the God who takes away our sins," is found in Psalm 99:8 and speaks of God's people: "You were to them God-Who-Forgives."

1. Underline a phrase that is meaningful to you from Psalm 25:16–18 below:

> Turn Yourself to me, and have mercy on me, for I am desolate and afflicted. The troubles of my heart have enlarged; bring me out of my distresses! Look on my affliction and my pain, and forgive all my sins.

2. When the Egyptians mistreated the children of Israel, how did God encourage His children in Psalm 99:8–9?

3. What have you learned about *El Nasa* (the God who forgives) this week that you can apply to your life?

    A. What do you most need forgiveness for this week?

    B. Talk to your leader about this situation. Receive and apply God's forgiveness once and for all.

C. Look up the promise associated with *El Nasa* in the following verses, and record what blesses you most.

Psalm 86:5:

1 John 1:9–10:

His name is *El Nasa*—His name is Jesus!

## EL AHAVA—GOD WHO LOVES

Another name for Jesus is *El Ahava*—"the God who loves." While this name doesn't actually appear in Scripture, it is a biblical way of describing the God who "so loved the world that He gave His only begotten Son, that whoever believes in Him should not perish but have everlasting life" (John 3:16). The name *El Ahava* is formed from the Hebrew word *aheb*, "to love," found in Deuteronomy 23:5: "The Lord your God turned the curse into a blessing for you, because the Lord your God *loves* you."

In Romans 5:6–8 we see the love of God further demonstrated on mankind's behalf:

*Every priest stands ministering daily and offering repeatedly the same sacrifices, which can never take away sins. But this Man, after He had offered one sacrifice for sins forever, sat down at the right hand of God, from that time waiting till His enemies are made His footstool. For by one offering He has perfected forever those who are being sanctified. But the Holy Spirit also witnesses to us; for after He had said before, "This is the covenant that I will make with them after those days, says the* Lord: *I will put My laws into their hearts, and in their minds I will write them," then He adds, "Their sins and their lawless deeds I will remember no more." Now where there is remission of these, there is no longer an offering for sin.*

**Hebrews 10:11–18**

When we were still without strength, in due time Christ died for the ungodly. For scarcely for a righteous man will one die; yet perhaps for a good man someone would even dare to die. But God demonstrates His own love toward us, in *that while we were still sinners, Christ died for us.*

1. From the above passage, record what stands out to you most, and why.

2. According to 1 John 4:19, how are you able to love Jesus?

3. Look up the promise associated with *El Ahava* in the following verses, and record what ministers to you most today.

    Jeremiah 31:3:

Isaiah 43:4:

*I have blotted out, like a thick cloud, your transgressions, and like a cloud, your sins. Return to Me, for I have redeemed you.*

**Isaiah 44:22**

His name is *El Ahava*—His name is Jesus!

## NAMES OF GOD REVIEW

1. Jesus is *Jehovah Tsidqenuw*—the Lord our righteousness. How does knowing that He has provided all the righteousness you need to stand before Him impact your life today?

2. Jesus is *El Nasa*—the God who forgives. What have you learned about *El Nasa* that you did not realize before this study?

3. Jesus is *El Ahava*—the God who loves. What is it that impacts you most about the love that God has for you?

4. Which biblical example were you most able to relate to this week—Gomer, Adam and Eve, or David? Explain.

*If You, LORD, should mark iniquities, O Lord, who could stand? But there is forgiveness with You, that You may be feared. I wait for the LORD, my soul waits, and in His word I do hope. My soul waits for the LORD more than those who watch for the morning— yes, more than those who watch for the morning.*

**Psalm 130:3–6**

5. How does knowing Jesus as *Jehovah Tsidqenuw, El Nasa,* or *El Ahava* help you today in your situation?

His name is *Elohim*—God our Creator.

His name is *El Elyon*—God Most High.

His name is *El Shaddai*—God Almighty, our gatekeeper.

His name is *Jehovah Tsidqenuw*—the Lord our righteousness.

His name is *El Nasa*—God who forgives.

His name is *El Ahava*—God who loves.

His name is Jesus!

# TOUCHED AND TRANSFORMED IN BROKENNESS

*Whoever falls on that stone will be broken; but on whomever it falls,*
*it will grind him to powder.*
Luke 20:18

### DAY 1: THE PROCESS OF BROKENNESS

When God touches a person's life, it produces humility and brokenness. Brokenness brings us to the place where we acknowledge God for who He is and finally relinquish control of our own lives. The world looks upon brokenness as a bad thing and upon broken things as worthless, but God always uses brokenness for His glory. It's only through brokenness that God is able to conform us to His image and work out His purpose in our lives.

Conforming is usually accomplished through applying external pressure to an object by pounding, molding, or shaping, much in the way a potter wedges clay. We are told in Jeremiah 18:1–4 that the Lord spoke to Jeremiah, saying,

> "Arise and go down to the potter's house, and there I will cause you to hear My words." Then I went down to the potter's house, and there he was, making something at the wheel. And the vessel that he made of clay was marred in the hand of

the potter; so he made it again into another vessel,
as it seemed good to the potter to make.

Isaiah 64:8 states, "O Lord, You are our Father; we are the clay, and You our potter; and all we are the work of Your hand." It is when we find ourselves in the hands of the Master that we are most open to the Holy Spirit speaking the Word of God into our lives and shaping us for His purposes.

As we are conformed to His image (see Rom. 8:29), Christ "through us diffuses the fragrance of His knowledge in every place" (2 Cor. 2:14). One way fragrance is diffused is through pressing. People press flower petals, fruits, and spices in order to release fragrance and precious oils. In much the same way, the sins of others, difficult circumstances, and unforeseen events press us, and it is in these times that God is able to diffuse the fragrance of Himself in and through our lives.

We see this in the life of Jesus, as He was pressed in the garden of Gethsemane, the place of His spiritual travail before His crucifixion. *Gethsemane* is a Hebrew word that means "the place where the olive is pressed" or "olive press." The ancient method of pressing oil was accomplished by the enormous weight of a gethsemane stone applying pressure to olives. The more pressure on the olives, the more oil produced. While Jesus was in the garden of Gethsemane, Luke 22:44 tells us that "being in agony, He prayed more earnestly. Then His sweat became like great drops of blood falling down to the ground." The tremendous pressure on Jesus was due to the fact that He, in a few short hours, would be scourged, mocked, ridiculed, beaten, falsely accused, and nailed to the cross for the payment of the sin of all mankind.

As we think of the concept of fragrance being brought forth from pressing, Jesus' death on the cross becomes life-changing. Ephesians 5:2 tells us that He has "given Himself for us, an offering and a sacrifice to God for a sweet-smelling aroma" so that we in turn, through the pressing and conforming of our lives, can be "the fragrance of Christ among those who are being saved and among those who are perishing" (2 Cor. 2:15).

In 2 Corinthians 1:8 Paul says he and his fellow workers were "burdened [or pressed] beyond measure." Then in 2 Corinthians 4:7–15 he continues,

> But we have this treasure in earthen vessels, that the excellence of the power may be of God and not of us. We are hard-pressed on every side, yet not crushed; we are perplexed, but not in despair; persecuted, but not forsaken; struck down, but not destroyed—always carrying about in the body the dying of the Lord Jesus, that the life of Jesus also may be manifested in our body. . . .
>
> All things are for your sakes, that grace, having spread through the many, may cause thanksgiving to abound to the glory of God.

*If through a broken heart God can bring His purposes to pass in the world, then thank Him for breaking your heart.*
**Oswald Chambers**

As Paul describes, there are many ways for a person to be broken, and unfortunately, being broken is not a one-time event. Sometimes pride needs to be broken as we realize how amazing God is and how unimpressive we really are. Sometimes, even *good things* need to be broken away from our lives so that we will relinquish our plans and agendas to God. Sometimes a person needs to be broken away from us so that God can have His rightful place in our lives. Paul goes on to tell believers in Romans 12:1–2,

> I beseech you therefore, brethren, by the mercies of God, that you present your bodies a living sacrifice, holy, acceptable to God, which is your reasonable service. And do not be conformed to this world, but be transformed by the renewing of your mind, that you may prove what is that good and acceptable and perfect will of God.

To present our bodies a living sacrifice means being willing to give up all our ideas regarding how we think things should be in our lives. It means being willing to be transformed by the renewing of our minds by the Spirit of God as He works in our hearts, allowing God to do things His way, even when it doesn't make sense to us.

1. Take a moment and allow God to search your heart. Ask Him to show you what He needs to break away from your life so that you can diffuse the triumphant victory of Christ to others. Look through the following list of circumstances. Can you identify with anything that is keeping you from diffusing the fragrance of Christ to others? Highlight what applies to you.

- Is your identity in what you do, where you live, in your family, in how much money you make, your career, or even in good things like serving the Lord? Anything less than finding your identity in Christ will produce odor and not fragrance!

- Are you preoccupied with personal image, overly concerned about your clothing, housing, cars, recreation, physical appearance, or any material goods?

- Do you spend excessive time on your phone, the Internet, social media, gaming, TV, etc.?

- Do you have a deceased family member or friend whom you cannot let go of?

- Do you have any relationship that you seek to control or that is difficult?

- Are you overprotective with your children or consumed with not being able to have children?

- Are you a perfectionist to the point of obsession?

- Do you have unrealistic expectations of others?

- Do you struggle with anything else? Explain below. Please realize that it doesn't have to be bad in and of itself.

*Rules for self-discovery:*

*What we want most;*

*What we think about most;*

*How we use our money;*

*What we do with our leisure time;*

*The company we enjoy;*

*Who and what we admire;*

*What we laugh at.*

**A. W. Tozer**

2. If your spouse or friends were to evaluate your master passion (what you hold dear), what do you think they would say?

*Before I was afflicted I went astray, but now I keep Your word. You are good, and do good; teach me Your statutes.*

**Psalm 119:67–68**

3. Has God begun the breaking process in your heart from these things? Are you able to see how God may be using this to draw you closer to Him? Explain.

### DAY 2: THE FRAGRANCE OF BROKENNESS

Victor Marx, of the ministry All Things Possible, wrote in *The Victor Marx Story,*

The unfortunate fact of life is that every human being experiences the good and the bad. The question is—how do we respond to the bad?

Look at it this way: Basically we can travel only two roads in life. One leads to eternal life.

The other leads to eternal death. One finds joy in loving others and doing good. The other becomes bitter by hurting others and by following sinful, destructive desires. One leads to God and an eternal family. The other leads to Satan and a lonely hell. It's easy to think you don't have a choice in life, when bad things in your past happened without your choice.

But you can't keep blaming others for the bad things that happened to you. Jesus can heal your wounds, but often the scars can remain as a reminder of how merciful Jesus is to love and heal your hurts. You can choose to let Jesus heal your past. You choose the road to life and to healing—it is not chosen by your parents or your abusers or by anyone else. I hope and pray that you choose the road to life.[1]

As we encounter the external pressures of this world, we can choose to be bad influences, diffusing the odor of bondage and death, or good influences, diffusing life, which is a sweet-smelling aroma to God. When we come to a place of brokenness, we will diffuse either the fragrance of Christ or the odor of self to those around us. What we diffuse is a direct result of our devotion to God or to self; without God conforming us, regardless of His method, we will diffuse the odor of pride and selfishness, which is of no use to anyone.

We can't have victory without battles; we can't have a

testimony without trials. God is faithful to turn our messes into messages that tell of the transforming work of His grace upon our lives. Just as a broken flask diffuses the fragrance of perfume, so too a broken life that abides in Jesus diffuses the fragrance of the triumphant victory of Christ!

When I think of a life of brokenness, I think of Jacob. Jacob had the promises of God, but he needed to trust God's timing instead of trying to take things into his own hands as well as ruining his relationships. Jacob's life shows that even when we have the promises of God, we can fall back into self-reliance, the exact opposite of brokenness. Jacob needed to be broken of his self-sufficiency before God could use him to the fullest.

In Genesis 32:24–31 we read,

Jacob was left alone; and a Man [the Angel of the Lord] wrestled with him until the breaking of day. Now when He saw that He did not prevail against him, He touched the socket of his hip; and the socket of Jacob's hip was out of joint as He wrestled with him. And He said, "Let Me go, for the day breaks."

But he said, "I will not let You go unless You bless me!"

So He said to him, "What is your name?"

He said, "Jacob."

And He said, "Your name shall no longer be called Jacob, but Israel; for you have struggled with God and with men, and have prevailed."

Then Jacob asked, saying, "Tell me Your name, I pray."

And He said, "Why is it that you ask about My name?" And He blessed him there.

So Jacob called the name of the place Peniel: "For I have seen God face to face, and my life is preserved." Just as he crossed over Penuel the sun rose on him, and he limped on his hip.

The Angel of the Lord was none other than God Himself. Jacob wrestled with God as God took him to the mat. This was because God needed to bring Jacob to a place of complete brokenness before Him. Jacob needed to be willing to accept God's will and ways for his life. God desired to do an amazing work through this man, but first He needed to take him from being Jacob, which means "heel catcher," "deceiver," or "governed by the flesh," to Israel, which means "governed by God." This was so Jacob would trust God to govern his life and let Him work things the way He saw fit.

This matter of self-sufficiency cost Jacob a great deal, including his relationship with his brother, Esau. Because Jacob had years before deceptively acquired Esau's birthright instead of waiting for God to give it to him as He had promised, Jacob had been forced to flee his home to escape Esau's wrath, and he had lived many years separated from his immediate family. The interesting thing is that when Jacob encountered the Lord in this wrestling match, he was actually on his way to meet Esau after more than twenty years of separation and unresolved sin between them. Now, having been broken in his encounter with the Lord, Jacob was completely humbled, and the result was that he sent out servants on the road ahead of him bearing gifts for Esau. He humbly blessed his brother, looking out for Esau's interests before his own. Spending time with God produced peace in Jacob's earthly relationships. It can do the same for us, no matter how damaged a relationship may seem to us.

Until we are broken before the Lord and allow Him to have His way in our life, we will continue to wrestle with Him and struggle to control our earthly relationships. Only when we come to Him in brokenness will we be governed by God and experience His peace. He is in charge, and His ways are perfect, having been established before the beginning of time! Isaiah 43:13 says, "Indeed before the day was, I am He; and there is no one who can deliver out of My hand; I work, and who will reverse it?" Any time we wrestle with God, it is futile; we are going to lose.

I am sure you can look back at times when you have thought you needed to help God out, only to realize that this is never a good idea. That is where Jacob found himself when he began wrestling with the Lord (see Gen. 32:24). God can and will do amazing things in our lives through brokenness, but even if we have been broken and have relinquished our situations and relationships to Him, we have a natural tendency to pick things back up again and wrestle with God regarding the details.

It took Jacob wrestling with God all night before he finally broke. I find it interesting that Jacob prevailed against the Lord to the point that God had to touch the socket of his hip and knock it out of joint. This caused Jacob to limp for the rest of his life as a reminder that God is in charge. Pastor Chuck Smith says that God wanted to crown Jacob, but first He had to cripple him.

I don't know what you are struggling with today, but know that you don't have to wrestle with God. Instead, you can choose to humble yourself under His mighty hand. He desires to bless and use you for His glory, but you must first be completely broken before Him, allowing Him to work when and how He chooses.

God is looking for availability through broken, humble lives. We can choose to let go and stop fighting against God. When we finally give up, God's Word becomes clear, and we are no longer ruled by fear, anxiety, or disappointment from temporal circumstances. When we finally come to the place of brokenness before God, we will be amazed at the things He can do through us that we could never do ourselves. When we understand that we can do nothing apart from God (see John 15:5) but can do all things through Christ who strengthens us (see Phil. 4:13), we will be able to rely on God and thus have peace even in the midst of a violent storm. Regardless of our situation, we can be blessed in knowing that God is with us: He is aware of and working out His will in all things. He is sufficient, and all His work satisfies!

There is always a price to pay when we don't simply trust God at His word. He is forced to step in and bring us to a place of brokenness. Please don't wait for God to give you a limp; allow Him to break you of your will, your desires, and your ways, not only in the big issues but also

*The devil, things and people being what they are, it is necessary for God to use the hammer, the file and the furnace in His holy work of preparing a saint for true sainthood. It is doubtful whether God can bless a man greatly until He has hurt him deeply.*

**A. W. Tozer**

*God never hurries. There are no deadlines against which he must work. Only to know this is to quiet our spirits and relax our nerves.*

A. W. Tozer

in how and when He works them out in your life. Know that the promise of Romans 8:28 is true—He is working all things out for good according to His will for those who love Him and are the called according to His purpose. Remember who God is, and let Him work.

## DAY 3: THE LIFE OF HANNAH

This week we will look at the life of Hannah. Spend time today prayerfully reading 1 Samuel 1:1–2:10 with the purpose of asking the following:

What do I learn about

- God/Jesus/the Holy Spirit?

- The lies of Satan?

- My situation?

- Myself/my beliefs?

- The truth of God's Word?

Is there

- A command or example in the passage for me to follow?

- A false identity I need to confess?

- A lie that needs replacing with God's truth?

- Something I need to repent of?

- A sin or judgment I need to avoid?

- Something I need to surrender and trust God with?

What especially ministered to you from this passage?

Respond to God by writing out a prayer.

From the reading of 1 Samuel 1:1–2:10 you just did, answer the following questions.

1. Who is Hannah's husband?

2. Who is Peninnah, and what did you learn about her?

*We are to look not at ourselves, our circumstances, our troubles, or the bumps in the road, but unto Jesus. Yes, the bumps are what you climb on!*

**Warren W. Wiersbe**

3. What do you learn about Hannah?

4. Hannah's sadness made Elkanah feel inadequate as a husband. Has your grief ever made others feel inadequate? How reasonable is it to look to others to fill the need in your life? Who alone can fill the longing in your soul?

People can often become discouraged, even depressed, when surrounded by difficult circumstances or relationships that are out of their control. When our focus is on these circumstances and conflicts, it produces sorrow. The remedy for this type of discouragement, anxiety, and depression is to look to God and trust Him with our situations, even when we don't understand. Then the Lord promises to turn our mourning to joy, comfort us, and make us rejoice rather than sorrow (see Jer. 31:13).

*If you look at the world, you will be distressed. If you look within, you'll be depressed. If you look at God, you'll be at rest.*

**Corrie ten Boom**

Hannah was a woman of sorrowful spirit, pressed to the breaking point because of her circumstances. Her husband, Elkanah, loved her, but she was sorrowful because she was barren. Hannah's sorrow was understandable; during Old Testament times, childbearing was an extremely important part of Middle Eastern culture, and children were a sign of success for the women who bore them.

Not only was Hannah barren, but she was also severely and continually provoked by Elkanah's other wife, Peninnah, who was able to bear children for her husband. Each year Elkanah took his two wives to Shiloh to present a sacrifice to God and worship the Lord at the tabernacle, and each year it was the same for Hannah, as she was provoked to misery by her jealous rival and constantly reminded of her emptiness that neither her husband nor anyone else could fill. It was in her brokenness that God was able to work a life-changing miracle in Hannah's heart.

*The secret is Christ in me, not me in a different set of circumstances. Until the will and the affections are brought under the authority of Christ, we have not begun to understand, let alone to accept, His lordship.*

**Elisabeth Elliot**

5. What is true barrenness, according to 2 Peter 1:5–11?

6. While barrenness is Hannah's issue on the surface, what do you think is the true reason for her anguish and sorrowful spirit?

7. Have you ever been so grieved that you believed the lie that God doesn't love you? If so, you may be a person who looks for physical evidence of God's love.

    A. Complete the following statement: "If God truly loved me, He would _____

_____

_____

_____."

B. Memorize Philippians 4:11–13. When you are tempted to believe lies, recall the truth of God's Word. What comfort do you find in verse 13?

Even in the midst of her brokenness, and in spite of the cruelty inflicted on her by Peninnah, Hannah made the trip to Shiloh for worship each year. Hannah didn't wait to clean herself up to enter the tabernacle; she entered with a brokenhearted spirit—bitter, unhappy, and defeated—and wept in anguish before the Lord.

8. What does 1 Samuel 1:9–10 tell us about Hannah?

A. Do you think you should wait until your heart is pure and your motives are right before approaching God? Why or why not?

B. Is it possible that you have been going through the motions of presenting your "sacrifice" to God and worshiping the Lord at the "tabernacle" while at the same time anguishing and sorrowing in spirit, perhaps even nurturing a root of bitterness? Take some time in prayer and ask God to help you trust Him with what concerns you.

If we waited for pure motives, none of us would make it even halfway to Shiloh. But if we choose to come to God, even with depressed hearts or bitter thoughts, God's grace can and will change us from the inside out.

## DAY 4: REMAINING FAITHFUL THROUGH BROKENNESS

Hannah's name means "grace and favor." In order for these beautiful qualities to be manifested through her life, Hannah had to be broken. It was through brokenness that her heart was changed and her faith refined as she called out to God, seeking His will.

At the lowest point in her life, Hannah went openly and boldly to God, pouring out her soul before the Lord (see 1 Sam. 1:15). It was at this point that she was able to ask specifically for her heart's desire as it lined up with the will of God. First Samuel 1:11 says that Hannah made a vow and said, "O Lord of hosts, if You will indeed look on the affliction of Your maidservant and remember me, and not forget Your maidservant, but will give Your maidservant a male child, then I will give him to the Lord all the days of his life, and no razor shall come upon his head." Hannah chose to focus on God and His provision instead of dwelling on her unchanging circumstances.

1. What are your tendencies when you suffer disappointment or pain? Are you prone to run away from the temple of the Lord and stop worshiping Him, or do you run to the Lord, offering Him your hurts? Explain.

2. As Hannah poured out her heart before the Lord, what was she accused of by Eli the priest, according to 1 Samuel 1:14?

3. Are you holding anything back from God because you are concerned with how others perceive you?

4. Satan tries to stop us from worshiping the Lord. He tries to keep us away from God's presence, like Peninnah did with Hannah, but the power of God's call is greater. God's purposes will prevail as they did with Hannah. Read Philippians 1:6. How does this verse encourage you today?

After speaking with Hannah, Eli realized that she was a God-fearing woman and blessed her by saying, "May the God of Israel grant the request you have asked of him" (1 Sam. 1:17, NLT). Hannah, after wrestling in prayer, came out the other side full of joy and renewed purpose (see 1 Sam. 1:18). Even though her circumstances remained the same at this point, Hannah was touched and transformed by God's peace as she relinquished her desires and circumstances to Him and chose to be satisfied with His will for her life.

Hannah eventually gave birth to a son named Samuel, once again proving that God keeps His promises.

5. Record the commitment we find in 1 Samuel 1:11 that Hannah made to God before she conceived.

6. Look up 2 Timothy 1:12, and write what ministers to you about this verse.

What a testimony! Hannah quickly learned to hold on to God's provisions loosely, recognizing that all things are God's and are best when given back to Him. She didn't argue with God or go back on her vow; instead she gave Samuel back to God willingly.

7. Have you ever been forced to give up someone or something to the Lord's will that you love dearly? Explain.

8. Do you currently have a "Samuel" that you need to commit back to God once and for all? Write out a prayer of commitment to God, and ask Him to fill you with His sufficiency.

Not only did God reverse Hannah's shame by making her a mother, but He also blessed her legacy. Hannah's faithfulness to God continued through her son, Samuel, who became a priest and was eventually used by God to anoint David as the next king of Israel. Hannah's faithfulness impacted her and her family—and an entire nation.

*I will restore to you the years that the swarming locust has eaten, the crawling locust, the consuming locust, and the chewing locust, My great army which I sent among you.*

**Joel 2:25**

I pray that you will not be satisfied to linger at the gate of God's presence, going through the motions of worshiping God while holding disappointments and bitterness in your heart. Enter into His inner courts of praise, coming before Him, desperately falling on your face before the One who alone can transform your brokenness. Count yourself blessed as one who has been touched by God's greatness and honored to extend His legacy however He chooses.

## DAY 5: THE NAMES OF GOD

As we continue our study in the names and character of God, today we will look at two names that speak to us of God's tender mercies toward those who are broken and in need of His healing and provision.

*Blessed be the LORD God, the God of Israel, who only does wondrous things! And blessed be His glorious name forever! And let the whole earth be filled with His glory. Amen and Amen.*

**Psalm 72:18–19**

### JEHOVAH RAPHA—THE LORD WHO HEALS

God said in Exodus 15:26, "If you diligently heed the voice of the LORD your God and do what is right in His sight, give ear to His commandments and keep all His statutes, I will put none of the diseases on you which I have brought on the Egyptians. For I am *the LORD who heals you.*"

When Moses led the children of Israel out of Egypt and crossed with them through the Red Sea, they wandered for three days in the hot, dry wilderness with no water. When they finally came to Marah and found a body of water, they couldn't drink, for the water was bitter. Can you imagine the disappointment? In typical manner, the people complained, as we all tend to do when we are disappointed. Moses sought the Lord; then out of obedience he cast a tree into the waters, and the waters were made sweet. The Bible says that God was testing Israel to see if they would acknowledge and trust Him—to see if they would be a fragrance to Him or an odor of self.

Ultimately, it was God who had led the people to the poisoned waters and what *appeared* to be a place of disappointment. Oh, what grief we could avoid if we understood and accepted that God is good and His ways are much better than we can ever imagine! We can be sure that *Jehovah Rapha* is able to heal body, mind, and soul. He is completely worthy of our trust, and when we do not understand why or how, we can always fall back on who He is and what we understand to be true about Him. In Isaiah 55:8–9 God tells us, "'My thoughts are not your thoughts, nor are your ways My ways,' says the LORD. 'For as the heavens are higher than the earth, so are My ways higher than your ways, and My thoughts than your thoughts.'"

1. It is important to understand that God is not bound by expectations, thoughts, man's timetable, or even common sense. List any disappointments you may have in your life today (kids, job, spouse, your life in general), and explain why you are disappointed.

*Trust in the LORD with all your heart, and lean not on your own understanding; in all your ways acknowledge Him, and He shall direct your paths.*

**Proverbs 3:5–6**

A. When you find yourself in a dry place that *seems* to be a disappointment, you may be facing a test, just as the children of Israel did. How can your disappointment be turned into praise?

B. Do you trust that God is able to deliver you? How would trusting God for deliverance affect your perspective?

2. God calls you to rise above your circumstances here on earth and to have a heavenly perspective. Write out 2 Corinthians 4:16–18, and underline what encourages you.

*You have turned for me my mourning into dancing; You have put off my sackcloth and clothed me with gladness, to the end that my glory may sing praise to You and not be silent. O LORD my God, I will give thanks to You forever.*

**Psalm 30:11–12**

3. When you don't know how things will work out, you can fall back on what you *do* know. God will deliver you and turn your bitterness into sweetness when you fully trust Him, because He is faithful. According to 2 Timothy 2:13, what is His faithfulness dependent on?

*Our vision is so limited we can hardly imagine a love that does not show itself in protection from suffering. The love of God is of a different nature altogether. It does not hate tragedy. It never denies reality. It stands in the very teeth of suffering.*

**Elisabeth Elliot**

4. Do you believe that you will ever be disappointed if you *abide in* and completely *trust* God? Why or why not?

His name is *Jehovah Rapha*—His name is Jesus!

## Jehovah Yireh—the Lord Will Provide

In Genesis 22 we learn of the name *Jehovah Yireh*, meaning "the Lord will provide."

The story begins in verse 2, where we are told that God tested Abraham and said to him, "Take now your son, your only son Isaac, whom you love, and go to the land of Moriah, and offer him there as a burnt offering on one of the mountains of which I shall tell you." Abraham knew the promise of God to make his descendants as numerous as the stars, yet here God was telling him to sacrifice Isaac, the son of promise. Though Abraham could not understand what God was asking, he was obedient by faith. We see this faith in verse 5, where Abraham said to the young men who accompanied them, "We will come back to you."

Genesis 22:6–13 tells us,

Abraham took the wood of the burnt offering and laid it on Isaac his son; and he took the fire in his hand, and a knife, and the two of them went together. But Isaac spoke to Abraham his father and said, "My father!"

And he said, "Here I am, my son."

Then he said, "Look, the fire and the wood, but where is the lamb for a burnt offering?"

And Abraham said, "My son, God will provide for Himself the lamb for a burnt offering." . . .

Abraham . . . bound Isaac his son and laid him on the altar, upon the wood. And Abraham stretched out his hand and took the knife to slay his son.

But the Angel of the LORD called to him from heaven and said, "Abraham, Abraham! . . . Do not lay your hand on the lad, or do anything to him; for now I know that you fear God, since you have not withheld your son, your only son, from Me."

Then Abraham lifted his eyes and looked, and there behind him was a ram caught in a thicket by its horns. So Abraham went and took the ram, and offered it up for a burnt offering instead of his son.

The Lord was testing Abraham, asking him to do what made no sense. As Abraham obeyed, the Lord met him in a way that he could not have expected. Because Abraham did not withhold his most cherished possession, the Lord provided a substitute for the sacrifice:

By Myself I have sworn, says the LORD, because you have done this thing, and have not withheld your son, your only son—blessing I will bless you, and multiplying I will multiply your descendants as the stars of the heaven and as the sand which is on the seashore; and your descendants shall possess the gate of their enemies. (Gen. 22:16–17)

Sometimes God just wants us to be *willing* to give up the things we hold dear that have a tendency to compete with the love we have for Him.

As we take steps of faith, trusting God and choosing

to obey, we will see God's provision for our situations. That is why in Genesis 22:14 Abraham called the name of the place "The-Lord-Will-Provide." God sent Jesus as the provision for our eternal life, and if we can trust God to provide us with eternal life, we can trust Him to provide us with what concerns us today in this temporal life. We must stop trying to finish in the flesh what was begun in the Spirit (see Gal. 3:3).

1. Why can you trust God, according to the following verses?

    Philippians 4:19:




    2 Peter 1:3–4:




In what state do you find yourself right now? Are you lonely? He is your companion. Are you broke? He is your provision. Are you anxious or fearful? He is your peace. Are you in bondage to something or someone? He is your deliverer. Jesus came to set the captives free! He will be whatever you need Him to be, so don't withhold yourself from Him. You can trust Him as *Jehovah Yireh*. He loves you and will provide all your need according to His riches.

*They returned, . . . strengthening the souls of the disciples, exhorting them to continue in the faith, and saying, "We must through many tribulations enter the kingdom of God."*

**Acts 14:21–22**

2. Write a prayer of thanksgiving to God for being your *Jehovah Yireh.*

His name is *Jehovah Yireh*—His name is Jesus!

## NAMES OF GOD REVIEW

1. Jesus is *Jehovah Rapha*—the Lord who heals. How does knowing that Jesus can heal all the barren areas of your life impact you today?

2. Jesus is *Jehovah Yireh*—the Lord will provide. How does knowing Jesus as *Jehovah Yireh* help you with your need?

3. Who could you most closely identify with during your study this week—Jacob, Hannah, Peninnah, or Elkanah? Why?

*Of one thing I am perfectly sure: God's story never ends with "ashes."*

**Elisabeth Elliot**

His name is *Elohim*—God our Creator.

His name is *El Elyon*—God Most High.

His name is *El Shaddai*—God Almighty, our gatekeeper.

His name is *Jehovah Tsidqenuw*—the Lord our righteousness.

His name is *El Nasa*—God who forgives.

His name is *El Ahava*—God who loves.

His name is *Jehovah Rapha*—the Lord who heals.

His name is *Jehovah Yireh*—the Lord will provide.

His name is Jesus!

# WEEK 5
## TOUCHED AND TRANSFORMED FOR SURRENDER

*Jesus said to His disciples, "If anyone wishes to come after Me, he must deny himself, and take up his cross and follow Me. For whoever wishes to save his life will lose it; but whoever loses his life for My sake will find it."*
Matthew 16:24–25, NASB

### DAY 1: GOD IS WORTHY OF OUR SURRENDER

It has been said that life is like a parade winding through the streets of a city. God's view of the parade is as if from a helicopter, where He can watch the entire parade all at once, with the beginning to the end in sight. Unfortunately, because we are limited by our physical bodies, we sit on the curb watching one float go by at a time, unable to see what is coming around the corner.

This is why it is important for us to "walk by faith, not by sight" (2 Cor. 5:7). We are not to rely on our own perspective but to trust that God knows what He is doing as He works out His sovereign plan for our lives. We have the difficult task of learning to surrender to His will for our lives and rest in His love, even though what we see may not make sense to us and may even be painful at the time.

In Psalm 139:14–18 David declares,

I will praise You, for I am fearfully and wonderfully made; marvelous are Your works, and that my soul knows very well. My frame was not hidden from You, when I was made in secret, and skillfully wrought in the lowest parts of the earth. Your eyes saw my substance, being yet unformed. And in Your book they all were written, the days fashioned for me, when as yet there were none of them.

How precious also are Your thoughts to me, O God! How great is the sum of them! If I should count them, they would be more in number than the sand; when I awake, I am still with You.

This psalm shows us a glimpse of God's sovereign love for each of His children. In Jeremiah 29:11 we are also told that God has "thoughts of peace" toward us to give us "a future and a hope," not to harm us or set us up for failure. God also promises that if we seek Him with all our hearts, He will be found by us. In Ephesians 3:20 Paul encourages us that God is "able to do exceedingly abundantly above all that we ask or think, according to the power that works in us." Not only does God know our names, not only does He have good thoughts toward us, but He also has plans for each of our futures, even down to the number of our days on this earth.

Perhaps you have wondered what this life is all about or wondered what your future holds and why God created you. Perhaps you were like me. When I accepted Jesus, I thought that instantly I would have a perfect life and live happily ever after. After all, wouldn't God bless me if I chose to follow after Him? That is what the enemy wants us to believe, and unfortunately, when things don't go smoothly or the way we think they should, Satan tempts us to question God's love.

Jesus tells us in John 16:33 that in this world we will have tribulation, but He also says that in Him we can have peace. God also promises in Psalm 16:11, through David's prayer to Him, "In Your presence is fullness of joy; at Your right hand are pleasures forevermore." We realize these promises of peace and joy as we choose to abide in Jesus and accept the work He desires to do in our heart. When we come to a place of absolute surrender with our plans, dreams, and ideas of how things should be, we will experience God's supernatural peace that passes understanding. We will begin to seek not our own plans but God's plan for our lives. Surrendering, while difficult, can be a freeing thing when we know that we are surrendering our lives to the God whose ways are perfect (see Ps. 18:30).

*The will of God is not something you add to your life. It's a course you choose. You either line yourself up with the Son of God . . . or you capitulate to the principle which governs the rest of the world.*
**Elisabeth Elliot**

Try to put yourself in the place of Mary, a young virgin, betrothed (promised to be married) to a man named Joseph. In Luke 1 we are told that during the betrothal, God sent the angel Gabriel to Mary in Nazareth. I am sure she had a variety of emotions as Gabriel appeared to her, saying, "Rejoice, highly favored one, the Lord is with you; blessed are you among women!" (Luke 1:28).

Mary was troubled by this greeting, but Gabriel said to her, "Do not be afraid, Mary, for you have found favor with God. And behold, you will conceive in your womb and bring forth a Son" (Luke 1:30–31). Mary, being a woman of the Word of God, knew that Gabriel spoke of the promise of God in Isaiah 7:14 that a virgin would conceive and bear a Son. Mary, being a virgin, asked the angel, "How can this be, since I do not know a man?" (Luke 1:34). Gabriel answered her, "The Holy Spirit will come upon you, and the power of the Highest will overshadow you; therefore, also, that Holy One who is to be born will be called the Son of God" (Luke 1:35).

Mary's response is a beautiful picture of surrender as she told Gabriel, "Behold the maidservant of the Lord! Let it be to me according to your word" (Luke 1:38). Mary understood that her position was not to dictate to the Master what she wanted but to accept His ways and timing. Mary agreed to a miraculous pregnancy that would be seen as suspicious, even scandalous, in a culture that believed in the death penalty for adultery. In spite of these circumstances, she sacrificially cried out, "My soul magnifies the Lord" (Luke 1:46). Mary represents an amazing example of complete surrender, teaching us what it means to fully trust in God and His Word, even when we do not understand it and even when it will be at great personal cost.

Imagine how Joseph must have felt at receiving the news that Mary was "with child of the Holy Spirit" before they were married or had had any sexual relations (Matt. 1:18). His reputation and that of the woman he was about to marry were in question before the community. Joseph could have had Mary stoned for adultery, but Matthew 1:19 says that he, "being a just man, and not wanting to make her a public example, was minded to put her away secretly." When an angel of the Lord appeared to him in a dream, saying, "Do not be afraid to take to you Mary your wife, for that which is conceived in her is of the Holy Spirit" (Matt. 1:20), Joseph had a choice to make. He could walk away in disbelief, concerned with what others thought, or he could trust God's word to him, believing that "with God all things are possible" (Matt. 19:26), and surrender his future plans to Him.

Surrender to God would become an important element in both Joseph's and Mary's lives. They needed to trust God not only with the virgin birth but also with the prophecies of Jesus' life and death. It must not have made sense as Mary later watched her son suffer and be crucified at the hands of wicked people. I don't believe any of us could fathom the pain of watching our child grow into a man only to be falsely accused, abandoned, beaten, and abused to death. Yet Mary had surrendered when the angel had appeared to her with the news of her pregnancy.

She also had the Word and promises of God: "You . . . shall call His name Jesus. He will be great, and will be called the Son of the Highest; and the Lord God will give Him the throne of His father David. And He will reign over the house of Jacob forever, and of His kingdom there will be no end" (Luke 1:31–33). His name was Jesus, the Messiah, the "Lamb of God who takes away the sin of the world" (John 1:29). In order to fulfill God's purpose for Him, Jesus must die in a specific way, according to God's Word. It was only by faith and the power of the Holy

Spirit that Mary was able to surrender her baby to death on the cross, because she knew that no word of God could be powerless against the enemy's schemes. Mary knew that God would absolutely perform what He said: Jesus would conquer death and defeat the grave once and for all.

Oftentimes God works in our midst in ways that are difficult, if not impossible, for us to understand in our limited view of eternity. Unfortunately, our tendency is to question, argue, become bitter, or even walk away from God when His ways don't line up with our understanding. The question for us to ask today is, do we believe that His words are true and will come to pass? If we answer yes and thus surrender to the plans God has for us, we too will be highly favored, the Lord will be with us, and we will be blessed. We will be highly favored children of God!

1. Look up Romans 11:33–36, and record what it says about God.

2. What from Romans 11:33–36 can help you when situations come into your life that you do not understand?

3. Read Ephesians 3:20. What can help you when you seem to be in an impossible situation?

## DAY 2: THE LIFE OF JONAH

For the remainder of this week, we will study the biblical character Jonah. Spend time today prayerfully reading all four chapters of the book of Jonah. Be sure to read with a purpose, asking yourself the following questions:

What do I learn about

- God/Jesus/the Holy Spirit?

- The lies of Satan?

- My situation?

- Myself/my beliefs?

- The truth of God's Word?

Is there

- A command or example in the passage for me to follow?

- A false identity I need to confess?

- A lie that needs replacing with God's truth?

- Something I need to repent of?

- A sin or judgment I need to avoid?

- Something I need to surrender and trust God with?

What stands out to you most about Jonah?

*The LORD sat enthroned at the Flood, and the LORD sits as King forever. The LORD will give strength to His people; the LORD will bless His people with peace.*

**Psalm 29:10–11**

Write a prayer in response.

Before we go further in our study of Jonah's life, it will be beneficial for us to define some of the terms found in the book of Jonah. Feel free to use a dictionary or use your own words to state what you know to be true regarding the following:

1. What is an idol? (The Hebrew word used for "idols" in Jonah 2:8 carries the idea of an unsatisfying vapor.)

*Those who pay regard to vain idols forsake their hope of steadfast love.*

**Jonah 2:8, ESV**

2. What is a prophet?

*Prophecy never came by the will of man, but holy men of God spoke as they were moved by the Holy Spirit.*

**2 Peter 1:21**

3. What is sackcloth, and what does it represent?

*You have turned for me my mourning into dancing; You have put off my sackcloth and clothed me with gladness, to the end that my glory may sing praise to You and not be silent. O LORD my God, I will give thanks to You forever.*

**Psalm 30:11–12**

*The sacrifices of
God are a broken
spirit, a broken and
a contrite heart—
these, O God, You
will not despise.*

**Psalm 51:17**

4. What is a sacrifice? You may want to look up Romans 12:1–2 to help you answer.

*The LORD's hand
is not shortened,
that it cannot save;
nor His ear heavy,
that it cannot hear.
But your iniquities
have separated you
from your God;
and your sins have
hidden His face
from you, so that
He will not hear.*

**Isaiah 59:1–2**

5. What is sin?

*The hour is coming,
and now is, when
the true worshipers
will worship the
Father in spirit and
truth; for the Father
is seeking such to
worship Him. God
is Spirit, and those
who worship Him
must worship in
spirit and truth.*

**John 4:23–24**

6. What is worship?

## DAY 3: THE SURRENDER OF JONAH

Nineveh was the largest city in the world in Jonah's day, and as the capital of a dominating empire, surely it was an intimidating place to go. In addition, the people of Nineveh were exceedingly wicked and brutal enemies of Israel. Yet because of God's love for all mankind, God called His prophet Jonah to go to this pagan Gentile city with the purpose of calling the people to repentance unto salvation.

Jonah, however, knew about the horrible deeds of these Ninevites all too well and desired God's punishment for them, not salvation. Knowing Jonah's heart, God spoke to him and told him to do two things: first, "Arise, go to Nineveh, that great city," and second, "Cry out against it; for their wickedness has come up before Me" (Jonah 1:2). In other words, God told Jonah to go to this city and expose its sin, call its people to repentance, and give the Ninevites a chance for salvation. The end of verse 2 is a great example of the character of *El Roi*, "the God who sees." None of man's wickedness is hidden before God; He sees it all, and sin may come to a point at which it demands the specific warning and judgment of God.

Rather than choose to surrender his own will and obey God, however, Jonah chose to flee to Tarshish (see Jonah 1:3).

1. Has the Lord ever told you to do something you didn't want to do? Explain.

2. Sometimes we don't like what God calls us to do. If we are honest, being forgiving, loving the unlovely, and trusting God when things don't make sense are all things we would probably rather "flee" from doing. How did Jonah attempt to flee the call of God, according to Jonah 1:3?

3. Jonah was told to do a difficult thing—something impossible in and of himself. What does Nahum 3:1–4 tell us about the people of Nineveh?

A. Why do you think Jonah did *not* want to do what the Lord told him to do?

B. While Jonah's disobedience may seem reasonable after understanding the wickedness of the people of Nineveh, that doesn't mean it was right. Are you justifying your disobedience to God's call to forgive, love, or reach out to someone because you have been a victim of sin? Explain.

*Oh, the depth of the riches both of the wisdom and knowledge of God! How unsearchable are His judgments and His ways past finding out! "For who has known the mind of the Lord? Or who has become His counselor?" "Or who has first given to Him and it shall be repaid to him?" For of Him and through Him and to Him are all things, to whom be glory forever. Amen.*

**Romans 11:33–36**

4. Is God's command to Jonah any different than the command God has given us from Matthew 28:19–20? Explain.

Jonah decided to go as far away as possible to escape God's call and presence. He found a ship going to Tarshish, a place thought to be at the end of the earth, which was in the opposite direction from Nineveh. Jonah allowed his bitterness, fear, and even his common sense to dictate his choices rather than trusting God in complete obedience. Jonah 1:3 tells us that "he paid the fare."

While Jonah was free to choose to step out of God's will, he would pay for his decision with dire consequences. The safest place for us to be is in the will of God. His Word is to be our guide always, and we must not depart from it under pretense of necessity, comfort, or circumstances. Any time we come up with excuses to go against what God is telling us to do, we are running from God, which is never beneficial, always futile, and often dangerous.

5. What does Psalm 139:7–10 say about escaping the presence of God?

6. When we think of Jesus, we often picture Him calming storms, but what did God do as Jonah tried to run from Him, according to Jonah 1:4?

*A storm is simply the hem of His robe, the sign of His coming and the evidence of His presence.*

**F. B. Meyer**

As Jonah sailed to Tarshish away from the Lord's presence, "the Lord sent out a great wind on the sea, and there was a mighty tempest on the sea, so that the ship was about to be broken up" (Jonah 1:4). The pagan sailors were afraid and began crying out to their gods, throwing cargo overboard to lighten the load. These pagan sailors were religious men, but only one man on board had a relationship with the true and living God. Through the storm God was calling out to Jonah. Jonah knew his God, he knew His Word, and he worshiped Him, yet in his indifference and apathy, even in the midst of danger to himself and the entire ship, "Jonah had gone down into the lowest parts of the ship, had lain down, and was fast asleep" (Jonah 1:5).

7. How does Romans 13:11–14 instruct believers?

*All around us there is tumult and storm, yet some professing Christians are able, like Jonah, to go to sleep in the sides of the ship. I want men of stern resolution, for no Christian is awake unless he steadfastly determines to serve his God, come fair, come foul.*

**C. H. Spurgeon**

In Jonah 1:7–10 we read that the sailors decided to cast lots to find the source of their trouble, and the lot fell to Jonah. The sailors asked Jonah a series of questions, and they "knew that he fled from the presence of the Lord, because he had told them." Jonah belonged to God, and although he was fleeing God's call on his life, God continued to pursue him. How ironic that even the sailors demanded that Jonah call on his God, when his only reason for being on that ship was to escape from God. Jonah knew his Savior but was still in need of deliverance.

It is important to understand that God is not punishing us when we encounter storms. Jesus willingly took our punishment at the cross. Rather, God wants to deliver us through our storms from the worldly things we hold on to that cause us to take our eyes off Him. This storm was about Jonah completely relinquishing his rights and fully surrendering to the call of God.

8. At this point in your study, is God revealing something to you that you need to surrender to Him completely? Explain.

9. Jonah told the sailors, "Pick me up and throw me into the sea; then the sea will become calm for you. For I know that this great tempest is because of me" (Jonah 1:12). As they threw Jonah overboard into the sea, the storm stopped its raging, and these godless Phoenician sailors "feared the Lord exceedingly." Their dread of the sea turned into the fear of Jonah's God, so they "offered a sacrifice to the Lord and took vows" (Jonah 1:15–16). In other words, it sounds as if these Phoenician sailors were converted! How does this speak to you in light of Genesis 50:20?

*Only being right with God will fill your soul to overflowing!*

**Margaret Ashmore**

## DAY 4: ALLOWING THE CROSS TO IMPACT OUR DAILY LIVES

Sometimes it takes being thrown into complete darkness and confusion with no direction, ability, hope, or comfort for a person to finally surrender to God. When the sailors threw Jonah into the sea, the storm ceased for them, but it only got worse for Jonah. In Jonah 1:17 we are told that "the LORD had prepared a great fish to swallow Jonah. And Jonah was in the belly of the fish three days and three nights." It took three days confronted with the pangs of death in the depth of the sea, in the most desperate time of his affliction, before Jonah finally surrendered and called out to God in prayer.

1. What has it taken for God to get your attention in the midst of your storms?

2. Who are you crying out to for help?

3. According to Jonah 2:1, "Then Jonah prayed to the LORD his God from the fish's belly." Finish the following statement from Jonah 2:2:

> I cried out to the LORD because of my affliction, _____
> _____ _____
> _____. Out of the belly of Sheol I cried, _____ _____
> _____ _____
> _____.

4. Look up the following verses, and record how God responds when we cry out to Him.

    Psalm 3:3–4:

    Psalm 30:2:

    Psalm 138:3:

5. Could something be keeping you from crying out to God today? If so, what is it?

6. Read Jonah 2:3–6, and record all Jonah's circumstances.

    A. Like Jonah, we can *feel* forsaken by God, but when such feelings come in like a flood, what should we do? According to Jonah 2:4, how did Jonah initially respond to his feelings?

    B. As Jonah's conscience was awakened to the abiding presence of God, he chose not to allow his feelings of despair to rule him. According to Jonah 2:7, what did he do instead?

7. In Jonah 2:8 on the next page, underline what you forsake when you fail to turn to the Lord for help.

Those who pay regard to vain idols forsake their hope of steadfast love. (ESV)

*Have we trials and temptations? Is there trouble anywhere? We should never be discouraged, Take it to the Lord in prayer.*

**Joseph M. Scriven**

As we walk with God, at times the cross of Jesus has a more forceful impact upon our lives than at other times. Often this occurs during difficult circumstances—some caused by the consequences of our own choices and some because of the sin of others.

The cross represents death, but it also represents victory. As Jesus hung on the cross, He cried out, "It is finished!" (John 19:30). In one act of complete surrender, He paid the penalty of sin on our behalf, defeated death, and conquered the grave, all for us. As we look to the cross, we are reminded that we too must *die to self*, fully surrendering to Jesus, who paid it all. When the cross impacts our lives, we will have a choice to make: run from it or surrender to it. We can choose to resist God or accept the path of surrender that leads to victory in Jesus.

True surrender always results in sacrifice. This is why Paul said in Romans 12:1, "I beseech you therefore, brethren, by the mercies of God, that you present your bodies a living sacrifice, holy, acceptable to God, which is your reasonable service." As a prophet, Jonah had committed his life to God, yet he faced circumstances and a calling he didn't want to fulfill. When Jonah finally came to the end of himself and realized that he could not fight the will of God, he remembered the vows that he had offered to God as His prophet. In Jonah 2:9 we read the end of Jonah's prayer to the Lord: "I will sacrifice to You with the voice of thanksgiving; I will pay what I have vowed. Salvation is of the LORD." Choosing to die to his own will and pride, Jonah offered a sacrifice of praise and thanksgiving, acknowledging the sovereignty of God and submitting to God's will for his life, whatever that entailed.

8. Could something be keeping you from surrendering to God today? If so, what is it?

*Let all those who seek You rejoice and be glad in You; and let those who love Your salvation say continually, "Let God be magnified!"*

**Psalm 70:4**

9. Can you relate to Jonah in that you don't *like* the circumstances you are in? What can happen when you allow the cross to intersect your life, according to Jonah 2:9–10?

God is never disappointed *in* us; He is disappointed *for* us when we chase after shadows. Oh, the ability, power, and influence we could have if we only looked to Jesus for everything! What grief Jonah could have avoided if only he had listened to God the first time.

In Jonah 3 we see God's longsuffering and mercy, as the word of the Lord came to Jonah again, giving him a second chance to respond to God's call. This time Jonah obeyed by going to Nineveh to preach God's message to that wicked society, telling the people that in forty days Nineveh would be overthrown (see Jonah 3:4). His obedience resulted in repentance and salvation for one of the largest, most corrupt cities in the world. In Jonah 3:10 we read that when God saw the repentance of the people, He relented from the disaster that He had said He would bring upon them.

Jonah 4:1, however, tells us that this merciful action of God "displeased Jonah exceedingly, and he became angry." Once again, Jonah allowed his heart to grow hard toward the people God had called him to love.

10. Imagine the blessing of knowing that God had used you to save an entire city. What did Jonah acknowledge about God in Jonah 4:2?

11. Read Jonah 4:3–11. What Jonah acknowledged with his mouth didn't line up with the selfish desires and expectations in his heart. List his actions from Jonah 4:3–9, keeping in mind that

God, in His mercy, had spared the entire city of Nineveh from judgment.

Verse 3:

Verse 5:

Verse 6:

Verses 7-8a:

Verse 8b:

*We will either flee the cross or die on it!*

**A. W. Tozer**

What does verse 9 tell us that God said to Jonah?

12. Have you ever been angry when God blessed someone you thought was undeserving? Explain.

A. After reading the book of Jonah, do you have a new perspective on why God chooses to bless others, even those you think are undeserving? Explain.

B. If your desires, like Jonah's, do not line up with God's character, ask God to change your heart. Ask Him to help you surrender everything to Him so that His perfect will can be worked out in your life.

*Pursue peace with all people, and holiness, without which no one will see the Lord: looking carefully lest anyone fall short of the grace of God; lest any root of bitterness springing up cause trouble, and by this many become defiled.*
**Hebrews 12:14–15**

## DAY 5: THE NAMES OF GOD

Why does God ask us to surrender to Him? Because according to His names, He is worthy of our surrender. He is a jealous God, like a husband who rightly desires to be the sole object of his wife's devotion, and He is also our Lord and Master, deserving of our total trust and obedience.

### EL KANNA—A JEALOUS GOD

The name *El Kanna* describes God's response to the sin of idolatry, which is forbidden in the life of a believer. The Lord Jesus is a jealous God who loves us with a perfect love that is unsearchable, and He desires our wholehearted response to that love. He is a consuming fire and will ultimately destroy anything in opposition to His holiness and anything competing for the love that is due Him. In Deuteronomy 4:23–24 we see a warning regarding this: "Take heed to yourselves, lest you forget the covenant of the LORD your God which He made with you, and make for yourselves a carved image in the form of anything which the LORD your God has forbidden you. For the LORD your God is a consuming fire, a jealous God."

We should not picture the jealousy of God to be like the jealousy of man. God's jealousy is a righteous zeal for the glory of His own name. This is why, in Exodus 20:4–5, God commanded His people not to worship or serve idols, saying, "You shall not make for yourself a carved image— any likeness of anything that is in heaven above, or that is in the earth beneath, or that is in the water under the earth; you shall not bow down to them nor serve them. For I, the LORD your God, am a jealous God."

1. God is a jealous God, meaning that He is jealous of anything that takes your attention and devotion away from Him. Reread Exodus 20:4–5, and record what God commands His people not to do.

Can you imagine being married and your spouse saying, "Just do whatever you want with whomever you want"? Would you feel loved if that were the case? It's no different with God. Because His name is *El Kanna*, we are able to see the depths of His love for us. In other words, He is so wholly devoted to us that He desires the same kind of love in return!

2. Thoughtfully write out Nahum 1:2–3. Underline the phrases in verse 2 that relate to *El Kanna*.

3. Record the first and greatest commandment in the Bible from Mark 12:29–30.

4. What warning are we given in 1 Corinthians 16:22?

5. What does Romans 1:24–26 say happened to those who "changed the glory of the incorruptible God into an image made like corruptible man" (Rom. 1:21–23) instead of glorifying God the Creator?

6. It is important to understand that God is not jealous *of* us but rather jealous *for* our affection. His jealousy is aroused when people or things take our focus and attention off Him. Ask God to show you if you are placing someone or something—good or bad—before your devotion to God.

    A. What is your master passion?

B. Spend some time asking God to help you place your affection on Him before anything or anyone else.

*I am the LORD, that is My name; and My glory I will not give to another, nor My praise to carved images.*

**Isaiah 42:8**

7. Think about your life today. How can you respond to the fact that God is high above the heavens, worthy of all wisdom, power, glory, honor and praise, yet loves you so much that He wants *your* affection?

*What is man that You are mindful of him, or the son of man that You take care of him?*

**Hebrews 2:6**

His name is *El Kanna*—His name is Jesus!

## ADONAI/YAHWEH/JEHOVAH/I AM—LORD, MASTER

*Adonai*, a parallel name to *Yahweh* or *Jehovah*, is translated "LORD." This name occurs more than six thousand eight hundred times throughout the Old Testament. We see this name in another form in Exodus 3:14–15, where God appeared to Moses and said, "I AM WHO I AM. . . . This is My name forever, and this is My memorial to all generations." While this name for God denotes His authority, it also carries a personal meaning. Our Lord and Master is not far off and uncaring but personal and active; He is near to and intervenes on behalf of those who love Him.

The amazing thing about this name, seen particularly in "I AM," is that it is an action word; in other words, God is the "becoming One." When an area of our lives is in desperate need, He will become whatever we need Him to be, because He alone is the source of supply for all our needs. Romans 11:36 says, "Of Him and through Him and to Him are all things, to whom be glory forever." Can you say that *Yahweh/Adonai/Jehovah*/I AM is Lord over all that concerns you today? He is either Lord of all, or He is not Lord at all. Take a moment and pray, seeking His touch for your life.

1. Look up the following promise associated with *Yahweh* from the following scriptures, and record what ministers to you most today.

   Proverbs 3:24–26:

Proverbs 18:10:

Psalm 91:9–11:

2. How does knowing that God's name is *Adonai/
Yahweh/Jehovah/*I Aᴍ help you in your situation
today?

> *If you believe
> in a God who
> controls the big
> things, you have to
> believe in a God
> who controls the
> little things.*
>
> **Elisabeth Elliot**

His name is *Adonai/Yahweh/Jehovah/*I Aᴍ—His name
is Jesus!

### NAMES OF GOD REVIEW

1. Jesus is *El Kanna*—a jealous God. How does knowing that Jesus is jealous for your affection impact your life personally today?

2. Jesus is *Adonai/Yahweh/Jehovah/*I AM—Lord and Master. How does knowing Jesus as *Adonai* help you trust and surrender your life to God in every situation that arises?

3. Who could you most closely identify with during your study this week—Mary, Joseph, or Jonah? Why?

His name is *Elohim*—God our Creator.

His name is *El Elyon*—God Most High.

His name is *El Shaddai*—God Almighty, our gatekeeper.

His name is *Jehovah Tsidqenuw*—the Lord our righteousness.

His name is *El Nasa*—God who forgives.

His name is *El Ahava*—God who loves.

His name is *Jehovah Rapha*—the Lord who heals.

His name is *Jehovah Yireh*—the Lord will provide.

His name is *El Kanna*—a jealous God.

His name is *Adonai/Yahweh/Jehovah*/I Am— Lord and Master.

His name is Jesus!

*From prayer that asks that I may be*

*Sheltered from winds that beat on Thee,*

*From fearing when I should aspire,*

*From faltering when I should climb higher,*

*From silken self, O Captain, free*

*Thy soldier who would follow Thee.*

*From subtle love of softening things,*

*From easy choices, weakenings,*

*(Not thus are spirits fortified,*

*Not this way went the Crucified,)*

*From all that dims Thy Calvary,*

*O Lamb of God, deliver me.*

*Give me the love that leads the way,*

*The faith that nothing can dismay*

*The hope no disappointments tire*

*The passion that will burn like fire,*

*Let me not sink to be a clod:*

*Make me Thy fuel, Flame of God.*

**Amy Carmichael**

# WEEK 6
# TOUCHED AND TRANSFORMED TO TRUST

*Trust in the LORD with all your heart, and lean not on your own understanding; in all your ways acknowledge Him, and He shall direct your paths.*

Proverbs 3:5–6

### DAY 1: TRUSTING GOD

Many people ask, if God is good, why do bad things happen to good people? The truth is, God is completely good. James 1:17 tells us that "every good gift and every perfect gift is from above, and comes down from the Father of lights, with whom there is no variation or shadow of turning." But because the world is in a fallen state due to the sin of Adam, others' sins can affect us in negative ways. God does not force Himself on any person, and that is why bad things continue to happen to "good people."

Because God is good, however, He will ultimately bring good out of bad situations. James tells us in James 1:12 that we are actually blessed when we endure temptation. When we resist a strong desire for things that are harmful or displeasing to God, we will receive the crown of life, which speaks of eternal rewards.

As we face temptations in our lives, it is vital that we realize they are not from God, for "God cannot be tempted by evil, nor does He Himself tempt anyone."

Instead, James explains, "each one is tempted when he is drawn away by his own desires and enticed. Then, when desire has conceived, it gives birth to sin; and sin, when it is full-grown, brings forth death" (James 1:13–15). While God does not tempt, God will test. The difference between tempting and testing is the desired result: Satan tempts us to set us up for failure and bondage; God tests us for growth in our spiritual dependence on Him.

*In You, O Lord, I put my trust; let me never be ashamed; deliver me in Your righteousness. Bow down Your ear to me, deliver me speedily; be my rock of refuge, a fortress of defense to save me.*

**Psalm 31:1–2**

Regardless of our trials, where we place our trust is vital. In John 5 we read about a man who had been infirm for thirty-eight years, unable to walk, who had been placing his trust in the wrong thing. This unnamed man made his way to the twin pools of Bethesda daily, where John 5:4 tells us "an angel went down at a certain time into the pool and stirred up the water; then whoever stepped in first, after the stirring of the water, was made well of whatever disease he had." This man desired to be made well, but only enough to want to get into the pool. Unfortunately, he had developed trust in the pool instead of the One who could make him well.

When Jesus came into the area, He approached the man and asked him an important question: "Do you want to be made well?" (John 5:6). Even more interesting is the man's answer: "Sir, I have no man to put me into the pool when the water is stirred up; but while I am coming, another steps down before me" (John 5:7).

When Jesus asked the infirm man, "Do you want to be made well?" the man was so fixed on the pool and his own personal limitations that he missed the impact of the question. Perhaps this man had grown comfortable in his infirmity; perhaps his condition had become his identity. Perhaps he wasn't comfortable in his situation but really didn't know how to rectify it. Whatever the reason, because of his misplaced trust, the man answered with an excuse, but "Jesus said to him, 'Rise, take up your bed and walk.' And immediately the man was made well, took up his bed, and walked" (John 5:8–9).

What an incredible display of God's mercy! Even though this man had put his trust in a pool of water, Jesus reached out to him and offered him the true freedom that could only come from trusting God. Whatever issues we struggle with, we must make a conscious choice to be made well, and we must also be willing to trust and surrender everything to Jesus. Like the infirm man at the pool, Jesus is asking us, "Do you want to be made well?" and, "Do you trust Me?"

*Oh, taste and see that the LORD is good; blessed is the man who trusts in Him!*

**Psalm 34:8**

The world we live in is full of sin, and no person is immune to it. Sin manifests itself in many ways but always causes pain, hurt, and heartache. The effects of sin touch every aspect of our lives and can hurt us in ways we could never have imagined. Regardless of whether we are dealing with the consequence of our own sin or are a victim to another's sin, the effects can, in some cases, hold our lives hostage.

Perhaps you have made poor choices in the past, resulting in harsh consequences. These poor choices must be repented of and committed to Jesus for His forgiveness, or the enemy will condemn you. The problem with any heart wound is that if it goes unchecked, the infection of the enemy's lies will lead to denial, anger, blame, bitterness, anxiety, depression, despair, anguish, shame, condemnation, and much more. These negative effects will eventually take root in our hearts, choking out the implanted word of truth. It is also important to remember that our lives always affect those around us, even though we may not realize it. "Do you want to be made well?" Jesus is asking. If we do, we must take ownership of our situation by asking God to forgive us for our past mistakes and sin so that our healing can begin.

It's easy to understand how our own sins bring consequences upon us, but what about when we are affected by someone else's sin? When this happens, it's easy for us to question the fairness of our situations and become resentful. Sometimes when we have suffered the consequence of another's sin, we start believing the lie that we must have deserved it or that God is punishing us. Of course this is not true. God loves us and wants us to trust Him with the consequences and subsequent emotions we experience as a result of someone else's sin.

Hurt, anger, and sadness are not sins; however, even if the hurt and anger are justifiable, these emotions can become sin in our lives if we do not handle them God's way. Hebrews 12:15 says, "See to it that no one falls short of the grace of God and that no bitter root grows up to cause trouble and defile many" (NIV). If we don't handle the hurt in our lives as God intends, turning it over to Him, we can become angry. Anger, if left festering, will

*You can make one of three choices when faced with a difficult situation because of your disobedience. You can blame God or someone else for your problems and try to cover up your sin; you can give up and return to your former, sinful life; or you can stand up, take responsibility for your actions, see God's forgiveness and trust in Him.*

**Warren W. Wiersbe**

eventually turn into bitterness, which acts like a poison in our lives. This poison is toxic not only to us but also to those around us. Bitterness can cause depression, anxiety, outbursts of anger, and many other consequences that tear us down and keep us from the abundant life God has for His children.

In Mark 3:5 Jesus was grieved in His Spirit and became angry, but He did not sin in His anger. He gave His anger to God and focused on doing good by healing a man with a withered hand. Ephesians 4:26–27 says, "'Be angry, and do not sin': do not let the sun go down on your wrath, nor give place to the devil." Notice that Paul does not say we cannot be angry; rather, he says that we must not sin in our anger. God created us with emotions, but He also knows that, over time, holding on to anger will destroy our joy in the Lord and make us ineffective witnesses for the gospel. Because our sin separates us from God, harboring sin in our hearts is like building a wall between us and God. We are the ones who build this wall, and we must be the ones to tear it down.

Last week we saw that God's name is *Yahweh*, I Am, meaning Lord or Master. Nothing touches our lives that I Am is not able to handle. Ephesians 1:11 tells us that Jesus is the one who "works all things according to the counsel of His will." Romans 8:28 also gives us great hope as children of God: "We know that all things work together for good to those who love God, to those who are the called according to His purpose." If we choose to trust God, He will use bad things for our good and for His glory

*Surely the arm of the* LORD *is not too short to save, nor his ear too dull to hear. But your iniquities have separated you from your God; your sins have hidden his face from you, so that he will not hear.*
**Isaiah 59:1–2, NIV**

169

to heal and redeem us to make us whole and set us free. As John 8:36 states, "If the Son makes you free, you shall be free indeed."

Ask God to show you if you have any bitterness or anger toward anyone. If you do, immediately deal with any negative emotions, giving them over to the Lord, so that the devil won't have a hold on you. Commit to pray for the person who has caused you or your loved ones pain, trusting that God will use it all for His glory. Regardless of what has caused your need for healing, you can trust the God who sees you. He is with you; He will heal those wounded areas of your heart if only you will let Him. When you trust your life to Him, He will use everything in your life for good.

As you finish this day's study, spend a few moments asking the Lord to reveal how people or circumstances are negatively affecting your life and how you may be negatively affecting those around you. Write out what God shows you below.

*The reason why many are still troubled, still seeking, still making little forward progress is because they haven't yet come to the end of themselves. We're still trying to give orders, and interfering with God's work within us.*

**A. W. Tozer**

## DAY 2: TRUSTING IN THE FINISHED WORK OF JESUS

As Jesus hung on the cross, His last words were "It is finished!" (John 19:30). This phrase is translated from the Greek word *tetelestai*, which means "to complete a debt or conclude a matter." It is equivalent to a cry of victory. In other words, Jesus completed His purpose for coming in the flesh, which was paying the debt we owed because of our sin. Jesus finished the work of reconciliation with God on our behalf, totally satisfying the wrath of God for us. This was a powerful fulfillment of Isaiah 53:3–5:

> He is despised and rejected by men, a Man of sorrows and acquainted with grief. And we hid, as it were, our faces from Him; He was despised, and we did not esteem Him.
>
> Surely He has borne our griefs and carried our sorrows; yet we esteemed Him stricken, smitten by God, and afflicted. But He was wounded for our transgressions, He was bruised for our iniquities; the chastisement for our peace was upon Him, and by His stripes we are healed.

1. What do the following scriptures say about sin and what God has done to rectify it?

    John 1:29:

Romans 3:23–26:

Titus 2:14:

2. Read 1 Timothy 1:15–16. What important truth did Paul come to realize about himself?

3. What is the effect of sin, according to Isaiah 59:1–2?

4. What is the penalty for sin, according to Romans 6:23a?

A. What contrast is found in Romans 6:23b?

B. In light of Romans 6:23, in what way should you view those whose sin has affected you?

5. Read the following passages to determine what you can do about sin.

Acts 3:19:

1 John 1:9:

6. What encouraging truth do you find in Hebrews 4:15–16 below that helps you in your circumstance today?

*Beloved, do not forget this one thing, that with the Lord one day is as a thousand years, and a thousand years as one day. The Lord is not slack concerning His promise, as some count slackness, but is longsuffering toward us, not willing that any should perish but that all should come to repentance.*

**2 Peter 3:8–9**

We do not have a High Priest who cannot sympathize with our weaknesses, but was in all points tempted as we are, yet without sin. Let us therefore come boldly to the

throne of grace, that we may obtain mercy
and find grace to help in time of need.

## DAY 3: THE LIFE OF JOSEPH

For those of us who believe in Jesus, our lives are not our own. Jesus has paid the penalty of our sin in full, and we belong to Him. But He has good plans for our lives, so we can trust Him. This concept is seen in the life of Joseph, Jacob's eleventh son.

Spend today prayerfully reading Genesis 37–50. Read with the purpose of asking the following discovery and response questions:

What do I learn about

- God/Jesus/the Holy Spirit?

- The lies of Satan?

- My situation?

- Myself/my beliefs?

- The truth of God's Word?

Is there

- A command or example in the passage for me to follow?

- A false identity I need to confess?

- A lie that needs replacing with God's truth?

- Something I need to repent of?

- A sin or judgment I need to avoid?

- Something I need to surrender and trust God with?

Write your findings below.

Write a prayer to the Lord in response.

*The LORD has anointed Me . . . to console those who mourn in Zion, to give them beauty for ashes, the oil of joy for mourning, the garment of praise for the spirit of heaviness; that they may be called trees of righteousness, the planting of the LORD, that He may be glorified.*

**Isaiah 61:3**

Joseph's ten older brothers viewed him as a spoiled tattletale who brought bad reports about them to their father, Jacob. This kind of behavior, combined with Jacob's open favoritism toward Joseph, caused the older brothers to be jealous and to resent Joseph to the point of hatred. To make matters worse, Joseph began relating dreams he'd had to his brothers—dreams that were actually prophetic visions of Joseph one day ruling over his entire family. The brothers' growing animosity toward Joseph led to an eventual plot to kill him in the wilderness. Reuben, the eldest of Joseph's brothers, objected to this plan. While this saved Joseph's life, Judah, another one of Joseph's brothers, sold Joseph into slavery. When Reuben discovered this, he was upset.

After carrying out this terrible plan against Joseph, his brothers returned to their father and deceived him into thinking that wild beasts had killed his favorite son. Unmoved by the unbearable grief of their father, these ten men continued their deception for the next twenty-plus years.

Joseph's brothers had sold him to a company of Ishmaelites, who in turn sold Joseph to Potiphar, an Egyptian officer of Pharaoh and captain of the guard. Joseph was probably only seventeen years old at the time. Though Joseph had every right to be bitter toward his brothers and his circumstances, he was not. Instead, he excelled at his duties and became one of Potiphar's most trusted servants, to the point that he was placed in charge of his master's household. God gave Joseph favor in the eyes of Potiphar, and Joseph prospered in all he did.

Potiphar's wife, however, tried to seduce Joseph. When he rejected her, she falsely accused him of attempted rape. Joseph was an innocent man, but Potiphar, believing the lies of his wife, had Joseph cast into prison.

During the years Joseph was in jail, he interpreted the dreams of two of his fellow prisoners. Both interpretations proved to be true, and one of the men was later released from jail and restored to his position as the king's cupbearer. Two years later, when the king had troubling dreams, the cupbearer remembered Joseph's gift of interpretation and informed the king of it. The king then called for Joseph and related his dreams to him. God again allowed Joseph to interpret dreams, and Joseph predicted seven years of bountiful harvests in Egypt followed by seven years of severe famine. He advised the king to begin storing grain in preparation for the coming drought. In recognition of Joseph's wisdom, the young Hebrew was made a ruler in Egypt, second only to the king.

Eventually the entire world was affected by the famine, including Joseph's family back home in Canaan. His father, Jacob, sent his ten oldest sons to Egypt to buy grain; only Joseph's younger brother, Benjamin, remained in Canaan. Upon arriving in Egypt, the brothers came face to face with Joseph, whom they did not recognize. His brothers bowed down to him while requesting grain, fulfilling the prophecy in Joseph's earlier dreams. Following a series of events, Joseph eventually revealed his identity to his brothers and forgave their actions that had so severely affected him. Jacob and his family moved to Egypt to be with Joseph, and Jacob's descendants stayed in Egypt for four hundred years until the time of Moses.

Joseph's story presents amazing insight into how God sovereignly works everything to bring about His plan in the lives of His people. Exactly as Romans 8:28 reminds us, "We know that all things work together for good to those who love God, to those who are the called according to His purpose."

When Joseph revealed his identity to his brothers, he spoke of their sin in this way: "Do not be distressed and do not be angry with yourselves for selling me here, because it was to save lives that God sent me ahead of you. . . . It was not you who sent me here, but God" (Gen. 45:5,

8, NIV). Later Joseph again reassured his brothers as he forgave them, saying, "You intended to harm me, but God intended it for good" (Gen. 50:20, NIV). Even though Joseph suffered greatly, he trusted God in the midst of his circumstances and could look back and clearly see God's hand upon his life.

We too can trust that God will work out our situations for good. Man's most wicked intentions can never thwart the perfect plan of God.

1. Read Genesis 37:18. Scripture says that God sees all things; why do you think, therefore, that He allowed Joseph to continue head on into such a deceitful plan by which he suffered betrayal and abandonment that included the loss of his family and home?

2. How did God use Reuben to spare Joseph's life, according to Genesis 37:21?

3. Can you name the people God has used, in a seemingly good or bad way, to preserve His plan for your life?

4. How does Isaiah 55:8–9 help you when you go through difficult times?

5. What is the evidence in Genesis 39:2 that the Lord was "with Joseph"?

6. Read Hebrews 13:5. Can you look back to a time in your life when you know that God was with you? How did He prove Himself faithful in your situation?

*In Him also we have obtained an inheritance, being predestined according to the purpose of Him who works all things according to the counsel of His will.*

**Ephesians 1:11**

7. According to Genesis 39:9, what was Joseph's reply to Potiphar's wife when she said, "Lie with me" (Gen. 39:7)?

A. What is the definition of sin, according to 1 John 3:4?

B. Lawlessness is breaking the law. Who wrote the law?

*He who covers his sins will not prosper, but whoever confesses and forsakes them will have mercy.*

**Proverbs 28:13**

C. In light of who wrote the law, who is *all* sin against?

## DAY 4: THE DISCERNMENT OF JOSEPH

Joseph's life seemed to be one long string of unfair and unwarranted events of victimization. Conspired against by his own brothers, taken from his home against his will, sold into slavery to a pagan land, falsely accused and imprisoned, Joseph could have easily questioned

God, doubted His goodness, blamed others, or perhaps wondered what sin he had committed to deserve such harsh punishment. Joseph, however, seemed to have an understanding of God that enabled him not only to survive under such harsh treatment but also to thrive in whatever situation he found himself in. Joseph was able to look at his circumstances as being orchestrated and used by God to bring about God's perfect plan.

1. Look again at Genesis 45:5. After Joseph revealed his identity to his brothers, how did he speak to them of their sin, which had had such great implications on his life? What attribute did he exhibit toward them?

2. How do you think Joseph was able to have this attitude?

*Finally, brethren, whatever things are true, whatever things are noble, whatever things are just, whatever things are pure, whatever things are lovely, whatever things are of good report, if there is any virtue and if there is anything praiseworthy—meditate on these things. The things which you learned and received and heard and saw in me, these do, and the God of peace will be with you.*

**Philippians 4:8–9**

3. The law of consequences is interesting. Consequences follow everything we do: our actions, our words, our thoughts. What does God call us to consider in Haggai 1:7?

    A. Look up Galatians 6:7–9, and write these verses below.

    B. Write a response to God in light of this passage.

4. Sometimes we can get stuck in the identity of victim, which skews our view of life. While another person's actions may have affected you in a terrible way, it is important to remember that "all have sinned and fall short of the glory of God" (Rom. 3:23). Read 1 Corinthians 4:4–5 below, and record what speaks to you from Paul's statement.

> My conscience is clear, but that does not make me innocent. It is the Lord who judges me. Therefore judge nothing before the appointed time; wait till the Lord comes. He will bring to light what is hidden in darkness and will expose the motives of the heart. At that time each will receive their praise from God. (NIV)

5. In what way do you think you have been a victim?

A. Do you believe you have been innocent in your situation? Explain.

B. If not, what part have you played in causing the consequences in your situation?

6. Do you honestly believe that God intends to use your circumstance for good? Why or why not?

7. Stop and think about it. Find at least one thing to write down regarding what God has done to show you His goodness in the midst of your trials.

8. Be honest with the Lord. Are you willing to let God do *whatever* He needs to do in your life so that He can use you for His purpose? Explain.

9. Record the rich benefits promised us in 2 Corinthians 4:16–18. Write a response to God in light of this passage.

10. Read Genesis 50:20–21. How does Joseph's response to his brothers minister to you, and how can you apply his response to your situation?

*Of course God will give us more than we can handle. That's what drives us to Jesus; that is the best thing that can happen to any of us.*

11. What promise can you claim from Lamentations 3:22–26?

*Many things about our salvation are beyond our comprehension, but not beyond our trust.*

**A. W. Tozer**

12. Chances are, throughout your life you will find yourself in distressing circumstances, some as unjust as those in Joseph's life. We learn from Joseph, however, that although not all things are good, "all things work together for good to those who love God, to those who are the called according to His purpose" (Rom. 8:28). In adverse circumstances you can be sure of His love for you. Romans 8:39 assures us that nothing "shall be able to separate us from the love of God which is in Christ Jesus." Since you know that God loves you, how should you act toward others, according to 1 John 4:7–11?

## DAY 5: THE NAMES OF GOD

It's not always easy to trust God, especially when we are in pain and don't understand what He is doing in our lives. But two more of God's names as revealed in His Word remind us that God loves us and desires the best for our lives. By getting to know these names, we will learn to trust Him completely for every aspect of our daily lives.

*Some trust in chariots, and some in horses; but we will remember the name of the LORD our God.*

**Psalm 20:7**

### EL ROI—GOD WHO SEES US

Have you ever been tempted with thoughts like "No one understands what I am going through" or "No one cares about me" or "If God loved me, He wouldn't allow this in my life"? In Genesis 16:13 God is introduced as *El Roi*, "the God who sees." As we learn this name for God, we can rest assured that God sees us even in our darkest trials.

As we discussed in week 2, God promised Sarai and Abram a son, but after years of waiting for that promise to be fulfilled, they grew impatient. When Abram lay with Hagar, Sarai's Egyptian handmaiden, and Hagar conceived, she despised her mistress, Sarai.

In her jealousy and spite, Sarai dealt harshly with Hagar, and when Hagar couldn't stand the mistreatment anymore, she fled to the desert. Genesis 16:7 says that "the Angel of the Lord found her by a spring of water in the wilderness, by the spring on the way to Shur." In the verses that follow, we see the Lord speak directly to Hagar's situation with words of kindness, comfort, guidance, and prophecy. Hagar was no doubt amazed that the Lord had heard her affliction (see Gen. 16:11).

1. Record what Hagar said as found in Genesis 16:13.

A. Stop and think about your situation. How does knowing you have a *God who sees* minister to you today?

*God does not hold you accountable for what others do to wrong you. But He does hold you responsible for how you respond. Love always anticipates and seeks the best in others.*

**Nancy DeMoss Wolgemuth**

B. Relate Romans 12:9–19 to Genesis 16. What do you see?

2. What do you learn from Hagar in this story?

3. What do you learn about God?

4. What do you learn about the effects of sin?

5. Look up the promise associated with *El Roi* in Proverbs 15:3 and 2 Chronicles 16:9, and record what blesses you most.

*Our light affliction, which is but for a moment, is working for us a far more exceeding and eternal weight of glory.*

**2 Corinthians 4:17**

His name is *El Roi*—His name is Jesus!

### JEHOVAH SHAMMAH—THE LORD IS THERE

The name *Jehovah Shammah* shows us another comforting characteristic of God that helps us trust Him: God is there. In other words, He is always with us.

We see this truth in the beginning, when God created Adam and Eve. The intimacy and trust between God and the man and woman He had created were beautiful. They dwelt in perfect, unhindered fellowship until sin entered the world through Adam, breaking their fellowship with God and with each another.

While God cast them from the garden, however, He didn't abandon them. Throughout history God's chosen people, although brought near to God, repeatedly chose to sin, turning their backs on the Lord. God, in His rich mercy, then repeatedly delivered them.

One example of God's faithfulness is found in Deuteronomy 4:37. God brought the Israelites out of bondage in Egypt, dwelling with His people in a pillar of fire and the cover of a cloud, leading them with His presence and strength. Unfortunately, God's people continued to sin, so the glory of the Lord departed from them.

Thankfully, the Lord never abandons His people. In Ezekiel 47–48 the prophet Ezekiel had a vision of the city of Jerusalem that must have given hope to his original readers who had once experienced God's glorious presence in their midst.

1. What does Ezekiel 48:35 reveal? What do you think this means?

2. According to Isaiah 41:10, what does God command? What does God promise?

3. While *Jehovah Shammah* is more the name of the city than a title for God (see Ezek. 48:35), it is closely associated with the idea of God's power and presence being with His people. What did Jesus say in Hebrews 13:5 that confirms this concept about God?

When we fail to realize that God is with us, it can cause fear and doubt. One time my four-year-old granddaughter was spending the night with us. As I slept with her in her room at our house, around three in the morning she started screaming due to a nightmare. I drew her close, wrapping my arms around her, and she said, "Hold me, Grandma." I reassured her by saying, "Shhh, Grandma is here. You are okay; I am here." She fell asleep almost immediately. That is exactly how God is: He is always with us, holding us, whispering in our ears, *"Shhh, I am here. You are okay; I am here."* How wonderfully comforting it is to know our God as *Jehovah Shammah*.

4. Where do you place your trust? Where is the first place you turn when you are afraid or upset? Be honest.

5. As you ponder the fact that He is *Jehovah Shammah*, ask yourself, "Is it enough for me to know that God is with me, always and forever?" Explain.

6. Rewrite 1 John 4:18–19 in your own words. What does this have to say about fear?

7. Look up the promise associated with *Jehovah Shammah* in the following verses, and record what blesses you most.

Exodus 33:14:

Isaiah 43:1–3:

8. How does knowing God this way change the way you view your circumstances?

*Let all those rejoice who put their trust in You; let them ever shout for joy, because You defend them; let those also who love Your name be joyful in You. For You, O LORD, will bless the righteous; with favor You will surround him as with a shield.*

**Psalm 5:11–12**

During difficult times, when you feel totally inadequate, weak, and gripped with fear, you don't have to be afraid, because God is with you. Completely trust Him, crying out, "Hold me, Jesus!"

His name is *Jehovah Shammah*—His name is Jesus!

## NAMES OF GOD REVIEW

1. Jesus is *El Roi*—the God who sees. How does knowing that Jesus *sees* everything that has touched, is touching, and will touch your life impact you personally today?

2. Jesus is *Jehovah Shammah*—His presence is with you. How does knowing Jesus as *Jehovah Shammah* comfort you and help you trust God with whatever is happening in your life?

3. Does knowing that God's presence is with you and will never leave you cast out your fear?

4. Who could you most closely identify with during your study this week—the man at the pool of Bethesda, Joseph, Joseph's father, Joseph's brothers, Hagar, Sarai, or Abram? Why?

His name is *Elohim*—God our Creator.

His name is *El Elyon*—God Most High.

His name is *El Shaddai*—God Almighty, our gatekeeper.

His name is *Jehovah Tsidqenuw*—the Lord our righteousness.

His name is *El Nasa*—God who forgives.

His name is *El Ahava*—God who loves.

His name is *Jehovah Rapha*—the Lord who heals.

His name is *Jehovah Yireh*—the Lord will provide.

His name is *El Kanna*—a jealous God.

His name is *Adonai/Yahweh/Jehovah/*I Am— Lord and Master.

His name is *El Roi*—God who sees us.

His name is *Jehovah Shammah*—the Lord is there.

His name is Jesus!

# WEEK 7
# TOUCHED AND TRANSFORMED TO WALK BY FAITH

*We walk by faith, not by sight.*
2 Corinthians 5:7

### DAY 1: MY TESTIMONY OF FAITH

Have you ever experienced a great day only to have it followed by struggle, disappointment, and hardship? Do you know what it feels like to be on a roller coaster of emotions? One day full of joy and hope, the next day fearful and shocked by circumstances beyond your control? Fear is the opposite of faith; fear paralyzes, while faith will propel us toward action. When we are fearful, we can choose to trust Jesus and walk by faith. To walk by faith is to walk in the fear of God more than the fear of man. Walking by faith means to live in light of the eternal, trusting God with the outcome of our lives.

My husband and I met and married shortly after we had both committed our lives to Christ. Early in the second year of our marriage, I became pregnant with our first child. We had not planned on starting a family yet, but we were excited to see what the Lord had in store for our future. Unfortunately for us, we made the mistake of believing that just because we had committed our lives to

Christ, we would have only good times and smooth sailing from that point on.

My first trial began when I went into premature labor and had to be hospitalized six weeks before my due date. God was faithful to us through a very difficult delivery, even though we had to leave our newborn son in the hospital due to complications.

I'll never forget the day our son could be brought home. At that time my husband owned his own construction company and had missed a lot of work due to the length of my hospital stay, so he went to work that day while my mom took me to pick up our son from the hospital. She dropped the baby and me off at our house to settle in, and I looked forward to my husband coming home to his new little family for the first time.

But as the hours passed into the evening without his arrival and with no word from him, I became concerned, since he was rarely late. Eventually a car pulled in the driveway, bringing my husband home. Clearly something was terribly wrong. When my husband came in, I learned that, on his way home from work, he had been in a car accident, totaling his pickup truck.

The next day things got worse. We received a phone call informing us that the other party involved in the accident had died and that there was a warrant out for my husband's arrest.

My heart sank, and my immediate response was "Why, God?" as though somehow God had caused this. My husband was heartbroken, not because of the warrant but because of the life that he felt responsible for taking. Nothing I could do helped; Clark desperately needed God's comfort. This was the beginning of circumstances that God used to deepen each of our relationships with Him individually.

Clark ended up having to serve time in jail, which was extremely difficult on both of us, but especially him. Again, I asked, "Why, God?" We both loved Jesus and had committed our lives to Him, so how could this be happening? I don't think I ever prayed more in my life than I did during that time we were apart.

We quickly learned that neither of us had any control over our situation. We could do nothing to make the circumstances change; we could only turn to the One who could get us through. He did that and more. Through those heart-wrenching times, God showed Himself faithful on our behalf time and time again, and I learned to trust Him in a way that I never would have learned otherwise. We saw Romans 8:28 become a reality in both our lives. God worked the situation out for good as each of us received His comfort in a way that would not have been possible in any other circumstance, as He built our testimonies, and as He enabled us to share with others and lead people to salvation. Everything worked out for good because of God.

Fast forward to our first son's birthday, and I found out I was pregnant with our second child. Again, we had not planned this, but after the initial shock we grew excited to see what God had in store, this time aware that there could be more trials ahead. This pregnancy was much better, the delivery much different, and I was able to take our second son home when I was discharged from the hospital. When I went in for my six-week checkup, however, I found out I had an aggressive form of cancer and would have to wean my son immediately and schedule surgery as soon as possible.

I was twenty-four years old. What would the surgery involve? Would I have to endure chemotherapy? How would I deal with two babies under the age of twenty-one months? Would I live long enough to see them grow up, marry, or have children of their own?

Because of the previous trial, we knew that God was faithful and that He was with us, but again our first reaction was, "Why God?" As so many questions swirled in my head, the Lord spoke powerfully to me from Romans 8:37–39:

> In all these things we are more than conquerors through Him who loved us. For I am persuaded that neither death nor life, nor angels nor principalities nor powers, nor things present nor things to come, nor height nor depth, nor any other created thing, shall be able to separate us from the love of God which is in Christ Jesus our Lord.

What assurance we have in knowing that if we have committed our lives to His care, nothing will ever be able to separate us from His presence. As we learned last week, His name is *Jehovah Shammah*—He is always with us, and not just us but with all those who belong to Him, even our loved ones, even our babies.

I had a choice to make. I could feel sorry for myself—and I felt as if I had every right to do so—or I could trust my Lord and receive His Word by faith, allowing His peace to wash over me. I had to decide if I wanted to *pout* or make my life *count*. The devil's priority is to isolate us from God and cause us to doubt His faithfulness. But when we turn to Jesus in difficult times, that is our first step toward victory. As I chose to receive God's Word by faith, my situation actually became an exciting venture as I asked God to show me every day how He would use my circumstances for His glory. It was a long journey, with much uncertainty, but I can say again that God is faithful. I had many opportunities in those days to share my faith, when people told me they didn't understand why I was so calm while facing cancer as a young mother with two little babies.

God eventually healed me, and I am alive today only because it is "in Him we live and move and have our being" (Acts 17:28). Our two sons are now grown with families of their own, and both Clark and I couldn't be more grateful to God for His healing touch on my life. I now realize that every day I have breath is a gift from God, and I want to make the most of each one for His glory. I want my life to count!

*Jesus answered and said to him, "What I am doing you do not understand now, but you will know after this."*

**John 13:7**

While we may not understand why things happen, and we may never understand a situation this side of heaven, two things we can know for certain: Satan will send temptations our way to try to trip us up and cause us to stumble as we get our focus on this life, but as our gatekeeper, God has filtered everything through His hands and only allows that which He will work for good, knowing that our faith will be strengthened if we trust Him.

It is important that we come to a place where our faith is not dependent upon our plans working out, our feelings, our limited understanding nor expectations. Instead our faith is in knowing who Jesus is, what He has done in the past, what He is doing now, and what He will continue to do. It has been said, "We don't know what tomorrow holds, but we do know who holds tomorrow." Just because we get through one trial does not mean there will not be another one soon to follow, but seeing God faithfully bring us through hardships serves to prepare us for what will come next and gives us cause to praise Him in every storm.

*All things are for your sakes, that grace, having spread through the many, may cause thanksgiving to abound to the glory of God.*

**2 Corinthians 4:15**

How do you feel when you are knocked to the ground? Do you throw a fit of anger, asking God why? Remember, we always have a choice: we can give in to Satan's temptation and our overwhelming feelings of fear and hopelessness, or, by faith, we can take God at His word. As we pray, we will see His faithfulness to us as He works everything out for His glory. The best part is knowing that He has chosen us to bring glory to Himself through these things, making us more than conquerors (see Rom. 8:37). Even though we might not feel much like conquerors in the midst of our hardships, we can stand on God's promise and claim the victory in Jesus' name.

1. What is your immediate response to hardships?

2. Can you look back on past experiences and say without a doubt that God had His hand on you and saw you through? Explain by writing out the testimony of what He has done to show His faithfulness and how He has revealed Himself to you. End your testimony by acknowledging what God has done to show His glory through your life.

*Our light affliction, which is but for a moment, is working for us a far more exceeding and eternal weight of glory, while we do not look at the things which are seen, but at the things which are not seen. For the things which are seen are temporary, but the things which are not seen are eternal.*

**2 Corinthians 4:17–18**

## DAY 2: FAITH IS FOUND IN JESUS

As we continue looking at the importance of walking by faith, spend time today prayerfully reading Matthew 14:1–36 about the ministry of Jesus with the disciples.

It had no doubt been a long and draining day. Jesus had just been told that Herod had beheaded John the Baptist. Matthew 14:13 states that "when Jesus heard it, He departed from there by boat to a deserted place by Himself." But as Jesus saw the crowds following Him, He was moved with compassion for them and healed their sick. That same evening, instead of sending the hungry crowd away, Jesus performed the miracle of feeding five thousand men with only five loaves of bread and two fish. If we counted women and children, the number of people could have been up to twenty thousand people, and the Bible says they all ate and were filled! What an incredible example of the compassion, power, and provision of God for His people.

When Jesus had satisfied their hunger, He sent the people away. No doubt Jesus and the disciples were physically exhausted after administering food and care to a crowd this size. In Matthew 14:22–23 we read how Jesus "made His disciples get into the boat and go before Him to the other side," and He then "went up on the mountain by Himself to pray." By His example, Jesus shows us the importance of getting alone with God in prayer. In order to do that, we must separate ourselves from the crowd and sit quietly before Him for intentional communication with our heavenly Father.

When evening came, Jesus was still on the mountain, but the disciples were now in the middle of the sea, their little boat tossed by the waves and wind. They were toiling, full of fear and anxiety; Jesus was no doubt praying, interceding on their behalf. Hebrews 7:25 tells us, "He is also able to save to the uttermost those who come to God through Him, since He always lives to make intercession for them." So often, like the disciples, we strive to the point of exhaustion, all the time forgetting that Jesus has not called us to toil but to rest. The disciples had just seen the miraculous feeding of the five thousand besides all the other miracles Jesus had done in their presence. Surely if Jesus could multiply the loaves and fish, He could deliver them and fulfill His intention to get them to the other side of the lake (see Matt. 14:22).

Matthew 14:25 says that in the fourth watch of the night, somewhere between three and six, Jesus came to the exhausted disciples' boat in the middle of the sea, walking on the water. As He approached their storm-tossed boat, they assumed He was a ghost and cried out in terror. But Jesus spoke directly to their fear: "Be of good cheer! It is I; do not be afraid" (Matt. 14:27). When we face storms in our lives, we need to remind ourselves that God has not given us a spirit of fear but of peace (see 2 Tim. 1:7). Though fear may be understandable in our particular situation, Jesus is far greater than any fear we can encounter.

Peter believed this as he said, "'Lord, if it is You, command me to come to You on the water.' So He said, 'Come'" (Matt. 14:28–29). Taking an enormous step of faith, Peter responded to the Lord's call, stepped out of the boat, and actually walked on the water to go to Jesus. What bold confidence in the Lord!

Yet immediately Peter's faith seemed to fade as he looked again to his situation. Matthew 14:30 tells us that "when he saw that the wind was boisterous, he was afraid." As Peter's focus shifted, his faith also shifted from a pure faith in God to a lack of faith due to the storm and the impossibility of his situation. But as Peter began to sink, he called out to Jesus, "Lord, save me!" (Matt. 14:30). Jesus does not expect perfection from His people, just dependence on Him and faith in His ability. He longs to hear the cries of His children for salvation! We see this in His response to Peter in verse 31 as "immediately Jesus stretched out His hand and caught him, and said to him, 'O you of little faith, why did you doubt?'"

Jesus gives us this same encouragement today. Even when we fail and start to sink, Jesus is there to rescue us. The danger is not the violence of the storm, the waves and winds that rage against us, or our trials and hardships but in a lack of faith. Peter knew who to call on at his moment of crisis, and we can too. Perhaps we have faith, but we need help to exercise it, like the man who cried to Jesus, "Lord, I believe; help my unbelief!" (Mark 9:24). Once we call out to Jesus, He takes us to the other side of our situation and calms the storms, resulting in our reverential awe of a miracle-working God that strengthens our faith in His ability. Then we, like the disciples, will come and worship Him, saying, "Truly You are the Son of God" (Matt. 14:33).

1. Do you have situations or circumstances today that cause you to doubt God's ability to work? Explain.

2. According to James 1:6, what is a person who lacks faith and doubts likened to?

3. Stop and think about the following questions. Be transparent in your answers, not writing what you think others would want to hear but answering honestly from your heart.

   A. Do you feel that God has ever failed you? Explain.

B. Has God abolished His promises?

C. Has God's Word changed?

D. Is there any situation too hard for God? If you think so, what is it?

4. Look up 1 Kings 8:56–58, and record all it has to say about the promises of God.

5. What does Peter call the promises of God, according to 2 Peter 1:4?

## DAY 3: A JEWISH RULER AND AN INCURABLE WOMAN

Spend time today prayerfully reading Mark 5:21–43 and the parallel account in Luke 8:40–56. These passages weave the stories of two very different people, both of them learning to walk by faith in desperate circumstances. Read with purpose, asking yourself the following:

What do I learn about

- God/Jesus/the Holy Spirit?
- The lies of Satan?
- My situation?
- Myself/my beliefs?
- The truth of God's Word?

Is there

- A command or example in the passage for me to follow?
- A false identity I need to confess?
- A lie that needs replacing with God's truth?
- Something I need to repent of?
- A sin or judgment I need to avoid?
- Something I need to surrender and trust God with?

Write your findings below.

Write a prayer to the Lord in response.

So many times we look to the testimonies of other people for hope. While testimonies can be encouraging, God is not bound by how He has worked in the past in others' lives or similar situations. It can be a trap for us to look to the method God has used in someone else's life or the way another person's trial has worked out. If we expect God to work the same way in our lives and He doesn't, we have a tendency to be confused, angry, or bitter. It is important to understand that Jesus does not work the same way in everyone's life. God works according to His will and knowledge of what is best for us as His children and for everyone else involved as well. His ways are not our ways; they are past finding out. That is why faith in God alone is so vital.

Jairus was a rich Jewish ruler of the synagogue who had only one child, a twelve-year-old daughter, and she was dying. Jairus came to Jesus, fell down at His feet, and begged Him to come to his house, saying, "My little daughter lies at the point of death. Come and lay Your hands on her, that she may be healed, and she will live" (Mark 5:23–24). Jesus agreed to go with him, and a large crowd followed, thronging them.

Also following Jesus in the crowd was a woman who suffered from internal bleeding. For twelve years she had turned to the world to deliver her from her infirmity, and it had changed nothing. Mark 5:26 says that she "had suffered many things from many physicians. She had spent all that she had and was no better." She had been left with no cure and no hope, but when she heard of Jesus, Mark 5:27–28 says that in her desperation "she came behind Him in the crowd and touched His garment. For she said, 'If only I may touch His clothes, I shall be made well.'"

1. Though this woman had nothing materially speaking, she did have one thing, and that one thing was the most important. In Luke 8:48 and Mark 5:34, what did Jesus say had healed the woman who touched His garment?

> *The apostles said to the Lord, "Increase our faith." So the Lord said, "If you have faith as a mustard seed, you can say to this mulberry tree, 'Be pulled up by the roots and be planted in the sea,' and it would obey you."*
>
> **Luke 17:5–6**

2. Was it the woman's *faith* or the *object* of her faith that made her well? Explain.

As the woman reached out and touched Jesus, she was healed immediately. When she told Jesus what she had done, "He said to her, 'Daughter, your faith has made you well. Go in peace, and be healed of your affliction'" (Mark 5:34). What a beautiful answer.

But "while He was still speaking, some came from the ruler of the synagogue's house who said, 'Your daughter is dead. Why trouble the Teacher any further?'" (Mark 5:35). The people around Jairus had lost all hope, knowing the girl was already dead, but Jairus didn't seem to care what others thought; in his desperation he held on to Jesus in faith. Mark 5:36 tells us that Jesus said to him, "Do not be afraid; only believe."

Taking Peter, James, and John with Him, Jesus followed Jairus to his house to see his daughter. When they came to the house, people were already grieving for the dead girl with loud weeping and wailing, but Jesus asked them, "Why make this commotion and weep? The child is not dead, but sleeping" (Mark 5:39). Because they had no faith and did not know the power of Jesus, they ridiculed Him, knowing that deliverance was physically impossible. They did not know, however, that with Jesus all things are possible (see Matt. 19:26).

Mark 5:40–42 tells us that when Jesus "had put them all outside, He took the father and the mother of the child, and those who were with Him, and entered where the child was lying. Then He took the child by the hand, and said to her, 'Talitha, cumi,' which is translated, 'Little girl, I say to you, arise.' Immediately the girl arose and walked, for she was twelve years of age. And they were overcome with great amazement."

Amazing indeed! Once again Jesus showed His power, command, and authority, this time over death itself. He also showed yet another example of His creative and varying methods of touching the lives of the individuals who need Him. The woman with the issue of blood was immediately and publicly healed as she reached out to Jesus herself. Yet Jairus's daughter actually died and was raised back to life privately as Jesus went to her on her father's behalf. This is encouraging, as it shows that we can call upon God for others' needs as well as our own, and it reassures us that He will always give us His uniquely personal touch that ministers perfectly to our specific situation.

It's human nature to compare our past or current situations with others'. As we compare Jairus and the woman, we can see many contrasts between these two very different people and their circumstances. Jairus had money, prestige, power, and people around him; the woman was the exact opposite: destitute, cast out, alone, and forgotten. Jairus's need involved a dearly beloved family member; the woman's need was deeply personal. Despite their stark differences, in their desperation both had enough faith to reach out to Jesus. In their deepest need they both made the personal choice to come to Jesus on their own, despite the doubters and naysayers surrounding them. In their vastly different situations, both understood that healing could come only from Jesus.

At the beginning of this week's study, I shared a bit

of my personal testimony as an example of how the Lord taught me to walk by faith in the situations I experienced early in my marriage and family. In many ways I can personally relate to each of the Bible characters we have just read about. Like Jairus, I came to God and interceded on behalf of my dear husband, asking God to heal him in the midst of his own personal trial, as he dealt with the pain of death. Like the woman with the issue of blood, I reached out to Jesus for my own physical healing from cancer. Like Peter, I had to step out of the boat and come to Jesus in the midst of the winds and waves of my own personal life storms—and I must continue to do so.

*Blessed is the man who trusts [and puts his confidence] in the LORD, and whose hope [and faith] is the LORD. For he shall be like a tree planted by the waters, which spreads out its roots by the river, and will not fear when heat comes; but its leaf will be green, and will not be anxious in the year of drought, nor will cease from yielding fruit.*
**Jeremiah 17:7–8**

Perhaps you can relate to my story or to the stories of others. Perhaps you still feel alone in your situation. Whether we can relate to others' personal testimonies or not, we can all relate to the reason and purpose for every testimony: to testify to the faithfulness, goodness, and glory of God. In spite of our varying or similar circumstances, the answer for each of us is always the same: the answer is always Jesus.

## DAY 4: REFLECTING ON FAITH

As we have seen in our readings this past week, faith is a vital part of our walk with God. In Hebrews 11:6 we read that "without faith it is impossible to please Him, for he who comes to Him must believe that He is" and that as *Jehovah Yireh*, God richly and graciously rewards those who seek Him, supplying all our needs. In Romans 12:3 the apostle Paul says that we are all given a measure of faith as a gift from God. We are not only saved by faith (see Eph. 2:8), but we are also called to walk by faith (see 2 Cor. 5:7).

While exercising faith is a choice we must make, the key is not the amount of faith we have but rather the object of our faith. Hebrews 12:2 states that Jesus is the author and finisher of our faith, and we must continuously look to Him so that our "faith should not be in the wisdom of men but in the power of God" (1 Cor. 2:5).

1. As you read about these incredible times when Jesus stepped into people's situations and did things that seemed impossible, what ministered to you the most?

   A. Why did that stand out to you?

   B. What difference will this week's lesson make in your life practically?

2. How has your faith increased as a result of this week's study?

A. Look up Hebrews 11:6, and record what it says about faith.

*By faith we understand that the worlds were framed by the word of God, so that the things which are seen were not made of things which are visible.*

**Hebrews 11:3**

B. How important is faith in God alone?

## DAY 5: THE NAMES OF GOD

As we have seen, God's names give us clarity about and confidence in who He is. Today we will look at another name of God, one that gives us strong reason to put our faith in Him and trust Him to take care of our concerns.

## JEHOVAH SABAOTH—THE LORD OF HOSTS

*Jehovah Sabaoth* is a title for God emphasizing His rule over every power in the physical and spiritual realms. More than 240 times in the Hebrew Scriptures, God is referred to as *Jehovah Sabaoth*, the Lord of hosts, who leads the armies of angels in heaven. This title speaks of God's power over all creation. God is able to use everything—angelic beings; men and women; sun, moon, and stars; rivers and oceans; mountains and deserts; heat and cold; wind and rain; all kinds of animals; even plants—for His purposes.

*Jehovah Sabaoth* afflicted the Egyptians with plagues using animals, insects, disease, and even a death angel because they dishonored His people (see Exod. 7–12). We see in Exodus 14 that *Jehovah Sabaoth* parted the Red Sea to deliver His people from the enemy and swallow up the enemy as they pursued the Israelites. In the book of Jonah, we see *Jehovah Sabaoth* cause a mighty tempest and use a great fish, a plant, and even a worm to get Jonah's attention and fulfill His purpose. In 1 Kings 18:38 we see that "the fire of the LORD fell and consumed the burnt sacrifice" of Elijah, proving to the prophets of Baal that *Jehovah Sabaoth* is God Almighty. In this week's lesson, Jesus reveals Himself to be *Jehovah Sabaoth* by walking on water, calming a storm, healing a woman of an incurable infirmity, and calling the dead back to life. The name *Jehovah Sabaoth* reminds us that we serve an indescribably powerful God and that all of creation serves His purposes.

1. We find the name *Jehovah Sabaoth* in 1 Samuel 17:45, in the story of David's encounter with

Goliath. Read 1 Samuel 17:22–51. As you try to put yourself in David's place, what are you able to relate to most?

When David approached the scene in the Elah Valley, he witnessed the army of Israel cowering in the presence of Goliath, the Philistine champion. As David stepped up to fight this giant, his brother became angry and accused him of being prideful. Even King Saul told David, "You are not able to go against this Philistine to fight with him; for you are a youth, and he a man of war from his youth" (1 Sam. 17:33). But David remembered how God had delivered him in the past and boldly replied, "Your servant has killed both lion and bear; and this uncircumcised Philistine will be like one of them, seeing he has defied the armies of the living God" (1 Sam. 17:36).

2. What did David conclude, according to verse 37?

3. How did David defeat the enemy, according to verse 40?

4. When Goliath saw David, "he disdained him; for he was only a youth, ruddy and good-looking" (1 Sam. 17:42). It would seem that all physical odds were against David. Record what verse 45 tells us about David's armor for this battle.

5. Even though all odds were against David in this seemingly impossible situation, what do verses 46–47 tell us what David's confident response to the enemy was?

   A. How could David say this about the future outcome of his battle as he faced this formidable enemy?

   B. There is no doubt that King Saul and the entire army of Israel knew the source of David's trust and confidence. While the above questions may be convicting, ask yourself, who do people see me trust in the midst of my battles? Do others see God's hand on my life when a giant is raging against me? Do I make sure that God is known rather than drawing others into sympathy for myself in my battle? If you don't like the way you answered any of these questions, spend a moment and confess that to the Lord, asking Him to help you by filling you with His Spirit. Ask Him to give you His perspective—one above your circumstances. Write out your prayer.

6. Do you currently have a Goliath in your life? Think about David and Goliath, and record the similarities between your situation and David's.

*Faith is an outward look. Faith does not look within; it looks without. It is not what I think, nor what I feel, nor what I have done, but it is what Jesus Christ is and has done, and so we should trust in Him who is our strength, and whose strength will never fail.*

**D. L. Moody**

7. If you belong to Jesus, you can be like David. When you encounter giants in your life (and you will), you can completely trust God's Word. God is *Jehovah Sabaoth*, and He reigns in power and victory. Read Isaiah 54:17 below, and note what it promises the children of God. Insert your name in place of the words "you" and "their."

"No weapon formed against _____ shall prosper, and every tongue which rises against _____ in judgment _____ shall condemn. This is the heritage of the servants of the LORD, and _____'s righteousness is from Me," says the LORD.

8. Maybe you feel helpless or weak or, at best, limited in your ability to handle what you have faced or

are facing in your life. As you finish your study this week, know that you are *not* defenseless, because the God of unimaginable power lives in you. As you seek to abide in Him and place your faith in God, then just as He is victorious, you too will be victorious. Read the following verse, and underline what ministers to you most.

> Be still, and know that I am God; I will be exalted among the nations, I will be exalted in the earth! The LORD of hosts [*Jehovah Sabaoth*] is with us; the God of Jacob is our refuge. (Ps. 46:10–11)

*Behold, He who keeps Israel shall neither slumber nor sleep. The LORD is your keeper; the LORD is your shade at your right hand. The sun shall not strike you by day, nor the moon by night.*

**Psalm 121:4–6**

You don't fight for victory; you fight from victory, because God is *Jehovah Sabaoth*, the Lord of hosts, the Lord of armies. He is our strength, our refuge, and our victory.

His name is *Jehovah Sabaoth*—His name is Jesus!

## NAMES OF GOD REVIEW

1. Jesus is *Jehovah Sabaoth*—the Lord of hosts, of heaven's armies! How does knowing that God is *Jehovah Sabaoth* help you in your situation today?

2. Who could you most closely identify with during your study this week—Peter, the disciples, Jairus, Jairus's daughter, the woman with the condition of blood, or David? Why?

His name is *Elohim*—God our Creator.

His name is *El Elyon*—God Most High.

His name is *El Shaddai*—God Almighty, our gatekeeper.

His name is *Jehovah Tsidqenuw*—the Lord our righteousness.

His name is *El Nasa*—God who forgives.

His name is *El Ahava*—God who loves.

His name is *Jehovah Rapha*—the Lord who heals.

His name is *Jehovah Yireh*—the Lord will provide.

His name is *El Kanna*—a jealous God.

His name is *Adonai/Yahweh/Jehovah/*I Am—Lord and Master.

His name is *El Roi*—God who sees us.

His name is *Jehovah Shammah*—the Lord is there.

His name is *Jehovah Sabaoth*—the Lord of hosts.

His name is Jesus!

# WEEK 8
# TOUCHED AND TRANSFORMED TO FORGIVE

*Be kind and compassionate to one another, forgiving each other,*
*just as in Christ God forgave you.*
Ephesians 4:32, NIV

## DAY 1: THE TROUBLE WITH FORGIVENESS

The key to understanding God's love for us is summed up in one word: "forgiveness." When we came to God and confessed our sins, He freely forgave our sins and gave us His gift of eternal life in Christ Jesus. Romans 5:8 tells us that "while we were still sinners, Christ died for us." Ephesians 1:7 further states that "in Him we have redemption through His blood, the forgiveness of sins, according to the riches of His grace." As we receive His forgiveness, we are free to extend that same forgiveness to others; but because love and forgiveness are based solely upon Jesus, we cannot offer them apart from His Spirit working in and through our hearts.

Forgiveness is a difficult subject for many of us. Even though we can personally know God as merciful and forgiving—and be thankful for our own forgiveness—practically we can run into roadblocks when applying forgiveness to those around us. Common questions we can find ourselves asking are, is forgiveness always necessary?

Am I required to forgive? Aren't some offenses too painful to forgive? Does forgiveness mean I have to trust that person again? Our sinful world overflows with examples of seemingly unforgivable actions, but God is willing and able to give us hearts of forgiveness for those whose sin has affected us.

One of the simplest reasons we refuse to forgive is that we just don't want to. Sometimes we would rather nurse our resentment and punish our offenders than forgive someone. Many times sincere Christians withhold forgiveness from others and feel completely justified in doing so. Their reasoning is that God doesn't forgive us without repentance; therefore, we must withhold forgiveness from others who have sinned against us until they properly repent. This is especially true with long-term conflicts that continue to surface. This thinking, however, couldn't be further from the heart of our Lord. Forgiveness is what God has given us in Christ, and He clearly asks us to offer it to others.

Refusing to forgive is choosing disobedience, and it will cause us to live in the misery of bitterness. If we refuse to forgive, our hearts will harden, and our willingness to forgive will decrease with each offense committed against us. It has been said that unforgiveness is like drinking poison yourself and then expecting your enemy to die from it. We may think we are exacting punishment on the one who hurt us, but in reality *we* are the ones who suffer spiritually, emotionally, and physically. Unforgiveness is a prison that keeps us in bondage, poisoning the healing that God wants to do in our lives and ultimately destroying us.

Saying "I *can't* forgive" is simply another way of saying "I *won't* forgive." Perhaps we have every reason to feel hurt, but we cannot effectively live our lives for the kingdom of God based on feelings. Forgiveness is a choice we make, often in spite of the pain from an offense. When we came to God and confessed our sins, He freely forgave our sins and gave us His gift of eternal life in Christ Jesus. This should cause us to have such an immense gratefulness and love for God that we want to offer others the same compassion, grace, and mercy He has given us.

*The fire of anger, if not quenched by loving forgiveness, will spread and defile and destroy the work of God.*

**Warren W. Wiersbe**

God did not create us with the capacity to carry the leftovers of all the pain and hurts from our past. We must give them all to Him in order to receive true healing. The Bible is clear in Hebrews 12:14–15 that we are to "pursue peace with all people, and holiness, without which no one will see the Lord: looking carefully lest anyone fall short of the grace of God; lest any root of bitterness springing up cause trouble, and by this many become defiled." God never asks us to trust people, only to love them. We are called to trust God alone, for He alone is trustworthy. Only as we trust God with our hurts and hearts are we able to reach out to others with His love and forgiveness.

1. When we realize that forgiveness frees us from pain and bitterness and is the only way to live an unhindered relationship with God and others, we will make it a priority in our lives, just as God does.

227

Write a prayer below, asking God for a willing heart to forgive today.

In Isaiah 43:18–19 we read God's words to the children of Israel, where He said, "Do not remember the former things, nor consider the things of old. Behold, I will do a new thing, now it shall spring forth; shall you not know it? I will even make a road in the wilderness and rivers in the desert." Just as He did for the children of Israel, God desires to do a new thing in our lives today, but we must first acknowledge our pain so that we can (1) seek forgiveness for our own sin and then (2) offer forgiveness to those who have hurt us. God desires to take back the territory of our hearts that the enemy has stolen from us through our own sin and our unforgiveness toward others. When God forgives us, we become free to forgive others— and also to pursue the new work God desires to do in and through our lives.

God's will for us regarding forgiveness is clearly spelled out in Ephesians 4:31–5:2:

Get rid of all bitterness, rage, anger, harsh words, and slander, as well as all types of evil behavior. Instead, be kind to each other, tenderhearted, *forgiving one another, just as God through Christ has forgiven you.*

Imitate God, therefore, in everything you do, because you are his dear children. Live a life filled with love, following the example of Christ. He loved us and offered himself as a sacrifice for us, a pleasing aroma to God. (NLT)

Keep in mind that forgiving others is not a suggestion but a commandment from the Lord. In Matthew 6:14–15 Jesus states, "If you forgive men their trespasses, your heavenly Father will also forgive you. But if you do not forgive men their trespasses, neither will your Father forgive your trespasses." This is serious business! If we refuse to forgive others, we are in no position to ask God to forgive us.

The good news is that God never commands us to do something that He doesn't give us the power to do through His Holy Spirit. When we receive Jesus as Lord and Savior, His Holy Spirit indwells us, teaches us, changes us, and empowers us to do God's will. We know through Scripture that His will is for us to forgive others as we have been forgiven, so we also know that He will help and enable us to do His will in this area of our lives.

*The fruit of the Spirit is love, joy, peace, longsuffering, kindness, goodness, faithfulness, gentleness, self-control.*

**Galatians 5:22–23**

Since forgiving others is a command from the Lord, it becomes for us an issue of obedience. We all struggle to obey at one time or another. When Saul halfheartedly obeyed God, failing to utterly destroy the enemy from among him as God had told him to, the prophet Samuel had harsh words for him: "Has the LORD as great delight in burnt offerings and sacrifices, as in obeying the voice of the LORD? Behold, to obey is better than sacrifice, and to heed than the fat of rams. For rebellion is as the sin of witchcraft, and stubbornness is as iniquity and idolatry" (1 Sam. 15:22–23). It's possible that some of us may struggle with disobedience in the area of forgiving other people.

2. Before this matter becomes a disobedience issue, what can you do?

3. Write out Jeremiah 42:6, and make it a sincere prayer right now.

4. Record what the following verses instruct believers to do.

Luke 6:37:

Mark 11:25–26:

*A whole lot of what we call "struggling" is simply delayed obedience.*

**Elisabeth Elliot**

Colossians 3:12–13:

Perhaps you are like Paul, who said, "I know that in me (that is, in my flesh) nothing good dwells; for to will is present with me, but how to perform what is good I do not find" (Rom. 7:18). You desire to obey because God is calling you to, but you are not sure how. You are not alone.

5. Record how you are able to obey God's Word, according to the scenarios and verses listed here.

A. God called Zerubbabel to rebuild the temple in Jerusalem after its destruction. He faced this daunting task among mountains of rubble with limited manpower. What did God say to Zerubbabel in Zechariah 4:6?

B. Obedience involves what, according to John 14:15–18? Record what Jesus said to the disciples that can also be applied in your life.

C. What have we been given for obedience, according to Romans 1:5?

6. God's grace is defined as the Lord's divine influence upon our hearts. His Spirit can be interchanged with His grace. In what way can His divine influence help us obey God when it seems impossible?

*Having been justified by faith, we have peace with God through our Lord Jesus Christ, through whom also we have access by faith into this grace in which we stand, and rejoice in hope of the glory of God.*

**Romans 5:1–2**

7. Write out the instructions given in 1 Thessalonians 5:15–22. Highlight what speaks to you most from this passage.

A. Do you believe that unforgiveness is a form of evil? Why or why not?

B. How does 1 Thessalonians 5:17 tell us to pray?

C. How does prayer help facilitate forgiveness?

Is God showing you that you need to have a change of attitude toward someone who has victimized you? Simply ask God if there is anyone in your life you need to forgive. If there is, write down the person's name, and begin to pray for him or her. The Lord may bring more than one person to your mind. You might not want to pray for a person who has deeply hurt you, but as you take this step of obedience, ask God to change your heart. Pray for the person every day, even if you don't feel like it. Keep a journal of your prayers, and record the change God makes in your heart.

8. When you find yourself in what seems to be an impossible situation, what does God promise you in His Word?

Philippians 4:13:

2 Corinthians 12:9:

*Joyful are people of integrity, who follow the instructions of the Lord. Joyful are those who obey his laws and search for him with all their hearts.*

**Psalm 119:1–2, NLT**

Ephesians 3:20–21:

## DAY 2: THE UNFORGIVING SERVANT

Today we will look at the parable of the unforgiving servant found in Matthew 18:21–35. Read this passage with the purpose of asking the following discovery and response questions:

What do I learn about

- God/Jesus/the Holy Spirit?
- The lies of Satan?
- My situation?
- Myself/my beliefs?
- The truth of God's Word?

Is there

- A command or example in the passage for me to follow?
- A false identity I need to confess?
- A lie that needs replacing with God's truth?
- Something I need to repent of?
- A sin or judgment I need to avoid?
- Something I need to surrender and trust God with?

Write out your findings. What stood out to you most?

Respond to God by writing a prayer.

*If you do not forgive men their trespasses, neither will your Father forgive your trespasses.*

**Matthew 6:15**

## DAY 3: THE NECESSITY OF FORGIVENESS

Jesus often taught in parables—earthly stories with spiritual meanings. In Matthew 18 Jesus used the parable of the unforgiving servant to give much-needed insight on the subject of forgiveness. He spoke of a certain king who wished to settle accounts with his servants (see Matt. 18:23). A deeply indebted servant owed this king ten thousand talents, which some say could be the equivalent of one billion dollars in today's economy. At any rate, it was an exorbitant amount, impossible to repay. The servant was brought before the king and begged his master for patience because he was facing a prison sentence for his debt. In a beautiful display of mercy and grace, the master chose to release his servant and forgive him the debt (see Matt. 18:27).

In verse 28 Jesus continued His parable, saying, "When that same servant went out, he found one of his fellow servants who owed him a hundred denarii, and seizing him, he began to choke him, saying, 'Pay what you owe'" (ESV). Despite his fellow servant's pleadings for mercy, the unforgiving servant refused to listen and threw the poor man in debtors' prison. When word got back to the master, he summoned the first servant and said to him, "'You wicked servant! I forgave you all that debt because you pleaded with me. And should not you have had mercy on your fellow servant, as I had mercy on you?' And in anger his master delivered him to the jailers, until he should pay all his debt" (Matt. 18:32–34, ESV). Ending His parable on a somber note, Jesus told His disciples, "So also my heavenly Father will do to every one of you, if you do not forgive your brother from your heart" (Matt. 18:35, ESV).

*Just as forgiveness is evidence of truly being forgiven, unforgiveness may be evidence that a person has never been impacted by the love of Jesus.*

In Jesus' parable the king represents God. The first servant represents us coming to Jesus the first time, unable to pay the debt we owe and in desperate need of mercy. Romans 3:23 says that all are debtors because all have sinned and fallen short of the glory of God. As debtors to God, we were not simply in need of patience from our Master; we needed total forgiveness. Just as the servant in the parable could not repay his debt, the debt for our sin could never be paid apart from the precious blood of Jesus. God, our merciful King, not only forgave our debt, but He also provided the perfect payment: the spotless Lamb of God who takes away the sins of the world (see John 1:29).

1. How does being reminded that your debt has been paid in full by the precious blood of Jesus make you respond to others when they sin?

*By grace you have been saved through faith, and that not of yourselves; it is the gift of God, not of works, lest anyone should boast.*

**Ephesians 2:8–9**

The second servant in Jesus' parable represents the person we need to forgive. This servant's debt was real, but it was very small in comparison to what the first servant owed the master. A hundred denarii were roughly equal to one hundred days' wages—a small fraction of the debt owed to the master by the first servant.

2. Look again at Matthew 18:28–30. After being forgiven, how did the master's servant respond to his own servant?

A. What do you think would cause this kind of response?

B. Could you be demanding *payment* from anyone (a debt of consequences for hurting you)? Pray that God would give you the mercy and grace you need to extend complete forgiveness to anyone who has hurt you.

*Forgive us our debts, as we forgive our debtors.*

**Matthew 6:12**

3. We are called to be Christlike in all our conduct, aware that others are watching us. Knowing that the master had treated the first servant with mercy and forgiveness, note the other servants' reaction in Matthew 18:31 as they observed the unforgiving servant's harsh treatment of his own servant.

A. Allow the master's words in Matthew 18:33 to resonate in your heart: "Should you not also have had compassion on your fellow servant, just as I had pity on you?" Sometimes we are blind to our own sinful conduct. Ask the Lord to reveal to you any lack of compassion you may have toward others, and write down what He shows you.

B. We must forgive others, no matter the sin committed. We must forgive because forgiveness is an attribute of our God, and we cannot represent Him accurately unless we become a person who reflects His character. If you have been unforgiving to others, write a prayer asking God to cleanse you of your unforgiveness and fill you with His love for others right now.

*We incur greater wrath by refusing to forgive than by all the rest of our indebtedness.*

**C. H. Spurgeon**

*"I say to you, her sins, which are many, are forgiven, for she loved much. But to whom little is forgiven, the same loves little." Then He said to her, "Your sins are forgiven."*

**Luke 7:47–48**

We do not stand in the same place as God, our King and Master, and we never can. Only God stands as the forgiver and source of all forgiveness. We, on the other hand, stand as those who have been forgiven and need continual forgiveness. Still, like our Master, we are called to forgive others. When we realize this truth, we will be far quicker to forgive without hesitation.

## DAY 4: FREEDOM THROUGH FORGIVENESS

God tells us in Psalm 55:22, "Cast your burden on the LORD, and He shall sustain you; He shall never permit the righteous to be moved." This includes the burden of having to forgive someone. As we saw earlier in this lesson, unforgiveness keeps us in bondage, gives the devil a foothold in our lives, and is the opposite of what God desires for us. God commands us to forgive others, and when we choose to obey Him and walk in forgiveness, we will live a life of freedom and victory. When we choose forgiveness, we are in God's perfect will, free to move forward to bring glory to God.

*It is for freedom that Christ has set us free. Stand firm, then, and do not let yourselves be burdened again by a yoke of slavery.*

**Galatians 5:1, NIV**

When God calls us to forgive, it does not mean that God is accepting of the sin that has been perpetrated against us; on the contrary, He hates sin. Forgiving others also does not mean that we must pretend that nothing happened, nor does it mean we have to trust the offender again. When a person's sin affects us and we offer forgiveness to them, it does not mean that we have to put ourselves in a situation for the trespass to occur again. We can truly love and forgive someone without being around that person. We are to use wisdom while obeying God, and we can rest assured that He will lead and guide us as to how we should interact with people who have hurt us as we walk in obedience to Him.

In this regard, it is important that we make a distinction between forgiveness and reconciliation. Whereas forgiveness can be one sided and is not dependent upon another person's actions, true reconciliation in a relationship requires repentance from one or both parties in the conflict and can only happen when both parties agree.

*Forgiveness.* As we have seen, true forgiveness comes from Jesus. Once we have received the forgiveness of God for ourselves, we can trust God enough to release other people to Him and show them the forgiveness that we have received. Forgiveness does not mean, however, that we must reconcile our relationship with our offender, possibly putting ourselves in harm's way again (especially in the case of sexual assault or physical abuse). Forgiveness simply means that we hold no bitterness or resentment against the offender. We are free to honestly pray for God's grace to be poured out on his or her life for salvation, spiritual growth, and blessing.

1. Explain forgiveness in your own words.

*Reconciliation.* We have all been born in sin, which separates us from God, and without receiving God's forgiveness for our sin, we can never be reconciled to a relationship with Him. So it is with our relationships here on earth. For reconciliation to be possible in a relationship, whoever sinned (whether one party or both) must express an honest admission of sin, seeking forgiveness from God and from the person sinned against. Both parties must be reconciled to God before they can be reconciled to each other, for only the *love of God* can cover any offense, and only the *grace of God* can give the necessary strength to restore a relationship based on forgiveness and love.

2. Explain reconciliation in your own words.

It's important to remember that forgiveness does not necessarily shield people from the practical consequences of their sin. For example, the owner of a car may forgive a man who steals his car, yet it is still appropriate for the car thief to be arrested and put in jail. As the thief repents and seeks forgiveness, he can be completely forgiven by

God, yet on a practical level, the man should be punished according to the law.

Sometimes in our limited perspective, an offender's consequences may seem either too light or too severe, but as we do our part to forgive and pray for the offender, we can trust that God knows best how to deal with each person. Even if the offender never appears to suffer any consequences, we can rest in the truth that *Jehovah Roi* knows and sees, and we can trust Him with the ultimate outcome. This knowledge frees us to love others without having to play judge and jury. At the end of the day, all sin is against God, and He is the perfect and just judge whom we can trust. Our part is simply to forgive.

3. Peter asked Jesus in Matthew 18:21, "Lord, how often shall my brother sin against me and I forgive him? Up to seven times?" What was Jesus' unexpected answer in Matthew 18:22?

4. Peter believed that he was being gracious by answering in the way he did. But Jesus, in essence, told him that we are to forgive others an unlimited number of times. As you think of all Jesus has forgiven you, what is your response?

*Repay no one evil for evil. Have regard for good things in the sight of all men. If it is possible, as much as depends on you, live peaceably with all men. Beloved, do not avenge yourselves, but rather give place to wrath; for it is written, "Vengeance is Mine, I will repay," says the Lord. Therefore "If your enemy is hungry, feed him; if he is thirsty, give him a drink; for in so doing you will heap coals of fire on his head." Do not be overcome by evil, but overcome evil with good.*

**Romans 12:17–21**

5. As Jesus hung on the cross, being crucified as a criminal, what does Luke 23:34 tell us that He cried out?

*We will never know the depths of God's love until we forgive someone who has not asked for forgiveness.*

6. Why are you required to forgive others if they are not sorry for hurting you, according to Mark 11:25–26?

*If we forgive in words only, but not from our hearts, we remain under the same condemnation.*

**C. H. Spurgeon**

7. List the instructions given in Colossians 3:12–14.

8. There is such freedom that comes from completely cleansing our hearts before the Lord. This freedom

is seen as we extend the forgiveness we have received from God to all those who have hurt us, those who are hurting us now, and those who will hurt us in the future. Referring back to the end of day 1 of this week's study, take the names you wrote down and fill in the blanks below, keeping in mind the words of Jesus in Luke 23:34. (Use a separate sheet of paper if you need more room.)

Dear God, I extend Your forgiveness to

_____ for

_____

_____.

Dear God, I extend Your forgiveness to

_____ for

_____

_____.

Dear God, I extend Your forgiveness to

_____ for

_____

_____.

Dear God, I extend Your forgiveness to

_____ for

_____

_____.

Dear God, I extend Your forgiveness to

_____ for

_____

_____.

Dear God, I extend Your forgiveness to

_____ for

_____

_____.

Dear God, I extend Your forgiveness to

_____ for

_____

_____.

*Search me, O God,
and know my heart;
try me, and know
my anxieties; and
see if there is any
wicked way in me,
and lead me in the
way everlasting.*

**Psalm 139:23–24**

8. Record what the following verses have to say about forgiveness and the treatment of your brothers in Christ.

Ephesians 4:30–32:

1 John 4:21:

9. What are Jesus' instructions to you in Matthew 5:43–48? Paraphrase this passage in your own words.

10. Consider all you have studied this week. Explain in your own words how it is possible to love or forgive your enemies.

*God does not hold you accountable for what others do to wrong you. But he does hold you responsible for how you respond. Love always anticipates and seeks the best in others.*

**Nancy DeMoss Wolgemuth**

## DAY 5: THE NAMES OF GOD

The last name of God we will examine in our study shows us that God loves peace. And this is the natural result of forgiveness—peace between us and God and peace among God's people. When we know that the Lord is a God of peace, it strengthens us to receive His forgiveness for our own sins and offer His forgiveness to those who have hurt us.

*I am the LORD, that is My name; and My glory I will not give to another, nor My praise to carved images.*

Isaiah 42:8

### JEHOVAH SHALOM—THE LORD IS PEACE

In Israel the Hebrew word *shalom* carries so much more meaning that our English word for "peace," going far beyond the idea of absence of conflict or anxiety. *Shalom* is a Hebrew covenant word meaning "tranquility." It denotes a peace that comes from completeness, wholeness, finished work, safety, or wellness, and in the Bible it expresses the result of God's faithful relationship with His people. This is something we can experience, but only as a result of placing our faith in the finished work of Jesus Christ on the cross. When we pray in the name of *Jehovah Shalom,* "the Lord is peace," we are praying to the source of all peace.

We find this name for God in Judges 6, where we see Gideon stressed to the point of terror as the Midianites were oppressing the nation of Israel. Gideon was hiding from the Midianites, threshing grain in secret because the Midianites had been destroying Israel's crops and greatly impoverishing the people. It was at this point, when Gideon's fear of the enemy was greatest, that God addressed him as a "mighty man of valor" (Judg. 6:12) and told him to go and save Israel from their enemy (see Judg. 6:14). What made Gideon a mighty man of valor?

Certainly not his bravery, strength, or confidence—not even his faith. Instead, in Judges 6:16 God told Gideon, "Surely I will be with you [*Jehovah Shammah*], and you shall defeat the Midianites as one man." (Remember, God is also *Jehovah Sabaoth*, the Lord of heaven's armies!) When Gideon feared for his life because he had seen the Angel of the Lord face to face, God said to him, "'Peace be with you; do not fear, you shall not die.' So Gideon built an altar there to the Lord, and called it 'The-Lord-Is-Peace'" (Judg. 6:23–24).

I love how God speaks to our precise fears and is able to bring peace directly into our situations—if only we will listen! As we walk with Jesus, we don't have to ask "Why, God?" or "How, God?" We need not fear. God tells us not to fear sixty-two times in the Bible because He has not given us a spirit of fear but of peace. It is Jesus who tells us in John 14:27, "Peace I leave with you, My peace I give to you; not as the world gives do I give to you. Let not your heart be troubled, neither let it be afraid." As we look at the world, the things we see can fill us with anxiety and trouble our hearts, but as we look to Jesus, our Prince of Peace, He will touch and transform our lives with a peace that surpasses all understanding (see Phil. 4:7).

*The Lord will give strength to His people; the Lord will bless His people with peace.*

**Psalm 29:11**

1. What does Isaiah 26:3 say about peace?

2. What does Jeremiah 29:11 say in regard to God's thoughts toward you?

    A. Do you believe that God's promise of peace means that this life will be full of ease and happiness all the time? Explain.

    B. What does John 14:27 say to adjust or confirm your answer?

3. How does Ephesians 2:14 support the definition of *Jehovah Shalom*?

His name is *Jehovah Shalom*—His name is Jesus!

## NAMES OF GOD REVIEW

1. Jesus is *Jehovah Shalom*—the Lord of peace. How does knowing that God is *Jehovah Shalom* help you in your situation today?

2. Who could you most closely identify with during your study this week—Saul, Paul, Zerubbabel, the unforgiving servant, or Gideon? Why?

His name is *Elohim*—God our Creator.

His name is *El Elyon*—God Most High.

His name is *El Shaddai*—God Almighty, our gatekeeper.

His name is *Jehovah Tsidqenuw*—the Lord our righteousness.

His name is *El Nasa*—God who forgives.

His name is *El Ahava*—God who loves.

His name is *Jehovah Rapha*—the Lord who heals.

His name is *Jehovah Yireh*—the Lord will provide.

His name is *El Kanna*—a jealous God.

His name is *Adonai/Yahweh/Jehovah/*I Am— Lord and Master.

His name is *El Roi*—God who sees us.

His name is *Jehovah Shammah*—the Lord is there.

His name is *Jehovah Sabaoth*—the Lord of hosts.

His name is *Jehovah Shalom*—the Lord is peace.

His name is Jesus!

*May the God of peace . . . make you complete in every good work to do His will, working in you what is well pleasing in His sight, through Jesus Christ, to whom be glory forever and ever. Amen.*

**Hebrews 13:20–21**

# TOUCHED AND TRANSFORMED BY THE HOLY SPIRIT

*We also glory in tribulations, knowing that tribulation produces*
*perseverance; and perseverance, character; and character, hope. Now*
*hope does not disappoint, because the love of God has been poured out*
*in our hearts by the Holy Spirit who was given to us.*

Romans 5:3–5

## DAY 1: ARE YOU LIVING IN THE FULLNESS OF THE SPIRIT?

My parents owned a gift store when I was in high school, and our entire family helped take inventory before the change of each season so that the ineffective items could be replaced with what was useful for the store's success. Just as a commercial store regularly needs to take inventory of its stock to determine which items are profitable or unprofitable, so we too need to allow God's Spirit to take inventory of our hearts to see if we are walking in the Spirit and living effectively for God's kingdom.

As we finish our time in this study, it is important that we continue to let God's Spirit touch and transform our lives. It's not always easy to ask the Holy Spirit to scrutinize our hearts; in fact, it can be quite painful and time consuming because He may want us to discard and replace some of our entrenched attitudes and behaviors so that our lives will produce the sweet-smelling aroma of God's love and forgiveness. The good news is that as we seek a touch from God's Spirit, He will be faithful to lovingly and gently reveal the things that are unfruitful in us and show us what is pleasing in His sight so that we can be filled with Him and thus exude His life and characteristics. As we seek His fullness in our lives, He will be faithful to touch and transform our willing hearts.

1. During this study, in which areas of your life have you felt the Holy Spirit's transforming touch?

2. Are you still struggling with something? Ask the Lord to do a complete inventory of your heart and show you what is unprofitable for your life spiritually. If you still struggle with certain issues, list them here, and take them to the Lord in prayer. Determine to leave them at the throne of grace so that you can be more effective for God's kingdom!

*Walk in the Spirit, and you shall not fulfill the lust of the flesh. For the flesh lusts against the Spirit, and the Spirit against the flesh; and these are contrary to one another, so that you do not do the things that you wish. But if you are led by the Spirit, you are not under the law.*

**Galatians 5:16–18**

We have covered a lot of ground in this study, but to go forward from here in power and victory, it is vital to live in the power of God's Holy Spirit. God has unlimited spiritual resources to pour out upon His people, but if we do not continually rely upon the Holy Spirit for daily living, we will lack His power and sufficiency.

Paul reminded the church of Galatia of this very issue in Galatians 3:3 when he said, "Are you so foolish? Having begun in the Spirit, are you now being made perfect by the flesh?" He also addressed this issue with the church of Corinth: "Not that we are sufficient of ourselves to think of anything as being from ourselves, but our sufficiency is from God" (2 Cor. 3:5). Jesus tells us that we can do nothing apart from Him (see John 15:5), but as we seek to be filled with the Holy Spirit, we will be enabled to live by His power. Paul wrote of this enabling power in Philippians 4:13, saying, "I can do all things through Christ who strengthens me." As we live in daily dependence upon His Spirit, He will give us the strength we need to walk in His power and victory.

So what does it mean to walk in the Spirit or to be filled with the Holy Spirit? In week 2 of our study, we saw that *Elohim* is the plural name for God (see Gen. 1:1). *Elohim* speaks of God the Father, God the Son, and God the Holy Spirit. The Holy Spirit is the third person of the Trinity and has all the elements of a person: He has a mind (see Rom. 8:27), He has a will (see 1 Cor. 12:11), He can be lied to (see Acts 5:3), He can be grieved or quenched (see Eph. 4:30), and He is our teacher (see John 14:26). His ministry can be described by three Greek words that demonstrate the varying work of the Holy Spirit in our lives.

The first word used to describe the Holy Spirit's ministry is *para*, meaning "to come alongside." Before we were saved or even aware that there was a God, the Holy Spirit *came alongside* us, calling us to Himself (see John 16:7–8). The Holy Spirit does this by gently making Himself known to us, sometimes in the subtlest ways— through other people, through circumstances, or simply

*No one can say that Jesus is Lord except by the Holy Spirit.*
**1 Corinthians 12:3**

through His creation. It is the Holy Spirit who convinces our heart that Jesus is Lord. If you are a believer in Christ, the Holy Spirit has already come alongside you and drawn you to salvation.

The Greek word *en*, meaning "in," expresses the second ministry, as the Holy Spirit *indwells* us at salvation. The moment we repent of our sin, acknowledge our need for Jesus, and ask Him to be our Lord and Savior, we are born again, and we receive the Holy Spirit within for salvation by faith. At this point we are also sealed with the Holy Spirit, who guarantees our salvation (see Eph. 1:13–14). Again, if you believe in Jesus Christ, you are indwelt by the Holy Spirit.

*Do you not know that you are the temple of God and that the Spirit of God dwells in you?*

**1 Corinthians 3:16**

The third ministry of the Holy Spirit is described by the Greek word *epi*, meaning "the coming upon," or "the overflowing," also described as the baptism with the Holy Spirit. Following the resurrection, Jesus met with His disciples to assure them that after His departure from earth to heaven, He would send the *Helper*, speaking of the Holy Spirit. Jesus then instructed the disciples to go to Jerusalem and wait for this promise of the Father (see Acts 1:4–8). In Acts 2:17–18 we read of the fulfillment of that promise. Peter was speaking of the *epi* when he told the Jewish believers, "You shall receive the gift of the Holy Spirit" (Acts 2:38). This third ministry of the Holy Spirit is available to all believers in Christ, although not all believers seek or embrace this ministry. Sometimes this is because they are simply unaware of it.

God is never bound by our methods, understanding,

or timeframes. This filling to overflowing, coming upon, or baptism with the Holy Spirit can take place at the time of salvation, as Acts 10:44–46 tells us it did when Peter took the gospel to the Gentiles for the first time. This baptism can also be a secondary experience, taking place after salvation, as seen in Acts 19:2–6, when Paul visited the church at Ephesus. When Paul asked the church members if they had received the Holy Spirit, they said they had not even heard that there *was* a Holy Spirit. It was the same with the church in Samaria, when Philip visited them (see Acts 8:14–17). Both groups were saved, but these believers in Ephesus and Samaria received the baptism with the Holy Spirit *after* salvation as He came upon them.

Once we have initially received the baptism with the Holy Spirit, we can go to the Lord on a continual basis, not to be baptized with the Spirit again but to ask for a fresh filling of His Holy Spirit for empowerment each and every day. When we do this, our spiritual lives will begin to take on an entirely new dynamic as we are "transformed into his image with ever-increasing glory, which comes from the Lord, who is the Spirit" (2 Cor. 3:18, NIV).

Being baptized with the Holy Spirit is available to you today. Like receiving salvation, you can receive the Holy Spirit by a simple step of faith with a heart that is ready to receive all that God wants to do in and through your life for His glory. The promise of Acts 2:38–39 is available to all of us: "Repent, and let every one of you be baptized in the name of Jesus Christ for the remission of sins; and you shall receive the gift of the Holy Spirit. For the promise is

*You shall receive power when the Holy Spirit has come upon you.*

**Acts 1:8**

*The Holy Spirit is the agent through whom God works today in the world, within the church and in individual believers. That is why we need to become well acquainted with the Holy Spirit, for He is the One whom the Lord has placed over the church to guide, direct, and empower its activities.*

**Chuck Smith**

to you and to your children, and to all who are afar off, as many as the Lord our God will call."

If you would like to be baptized with the Holy Spirit for the first time or have asked for this baptism in the past and need a fresh touch from God, He is waiting for you to call upon Him; when you do, He will be faithful to fill you to overflowing with His provision of grace. All you need to do is ask to "receive the promise of the Spirit through faith" (Gal. 3:14). Simply ask and receive, and thank Him for the gift of the Holy Spirit in your life.

*If you then, being evil, know how to give good gifts to your children, how much more will your heavenly Father give the Holy Spirit to those who ask Him!*

**Luke 11:13**

3. Having worked through this study and now considered the work of the Holy Spirit in your life, look back to week 1 of this study and review the list of symptoms and triggers that represent what the world has to offer. List some of the symptoms or triggers that you struggled with at the beginning of the study, and record how the Lord has worked in these areas of your life through the weeks of the study.

4. Contrast the lists from week 1 with a list of what Jesus offers when we allow Him to *touch and transform* our lives. Go through the following list from God's Word, highlighting some of the results of the Holy Spirit's influence as He comes alongside, in, and upon our lives. Circle those things you desire for your life and then pray over them, knowing that the Holy Spirit will be faithful to meet you today.

- The Holy Spirit convicts the world of sin, righteousness, and judgment (see Ps. 98:2; John 16:8).

- The Holy Spirit makes us spiritually alive (see Rom. 8:11; 1 Pet. 3:18).

- The Holy Spirit gives us access to God the Father (see Eph. 2:18).

- The Holy Spirit grants eternal life (see Gal. 6:8).

- The Holy Spirit reveals the deep things of God to us (see 1 Cor. 2:10).

- The Holy Spirit comforts us (see Acts 9:31).

- The Holy Spirit delivers us from fear and into adoption by Abba Father (see Rom. 8:15).

- The Holy Spirit reveals all that has been given to us from God (see 1 Cor. 2:12).

- The Holy Spirit frees us from the law of sin and death, bringing liberty (see Rom. 8:2; 2 Cor. 3:17).

- The Holy Spirit washes and renews us (see 1 Cor. 6:11; Titus 3:5).

- The Holy Spirit reveals Jesus Christ to us and in us (see John 16:14–15).

- The Holy Spirit fills and indwells us (see John 14:17; Acts 2:4; 4:8, 31; 9:17; Rom. 8:9; 1 Cor. 3:16; Eph. 5:18; 2 Tim. 1:14).

- The Holy Spirit regenerates us (see John 3:5–8; Titus 3:5).

- The Holy Spirit sanctifies us (see Rom. 15:16; 2 Thess. 2:13; 1 Pet. 1:2).

- The Holy Spirit transforms us into the image of Jesus Christ (see 2 Cor. 3:18).

- The Holy Spirit bears witness in us that we are children of God (see Rom. 8:16).

- The Holy Spirit leads us (see Matt. 4:1; Luke 4:1; Rom. 8:14; Gal. 5:18).

- The Holy Spirit empowers us (see Luke 4:14; 24:49; Acts 1:8; Rom. 15:13, 19).

- The Holy Spirit strengthens us (see Eph. 3:16).

- The Holy Spirit casts out demons (see Matt. 12:28).

- The Holy Spirit prays for us (see Rom. 8:26–27).

- The Holy Spirit teaches us all things and brings to our remembrance what Jesus said (see John 14:26; 1 Cor. 2:13).

- The Holy Spirit speaks to us, in us, and through us (see Matt. 10:20; Acts 2:4; 8:29; 10:19; 11:12, 28; 13:2; 16:6–7; 21:4, 11; 1 Cor. 12:3; 1 Tim. 4:1; Heb. 3:7–8; Rev. 2:11).

- The Holy Spirit glorifies and points everyone to Jesus Christ (see John 15:26; 16:14).

- The Holy Spirit teaches us to pray (see Rom. 8:26–27; Jude 1:20).

- The Holy Spirit anoints for ministry to others (see Isa. 61:1; Luke 4:18; Acts 10:38).

- The Holy Spirit enables us to know that Jesus abides in us (see 1 John 3:24; 4:13).

- The Holy Spirit produces in us the fruit (evidence) of His work and presence, which is love (see Gal. 5:22–23).

- The Holy Spirit distributes various spiritual gifts and manifestations (outward workings) of His presence to and through the body as He wills (see 1 Cor. 12:4, 8–11; Eph. 4:7–8; Heb. 2:4).

- The Holy Spirit brings unity to the body of Christ (the church). Just as the members of the Godhead are one, we too are united as one in the Holy Spirit as we abide in Jesus (see Eph. 2:14–18; 4:3–6). Therefore the primary evidences of the Holy Spirit working in a group are love and unity (see 1 Cor. 13).

- The Holy Spirit pours out God's love into our hearts, bringing hope (see Rom. 5:5).

- The Holy Spirit seals us until the day of redemption (see Eph. 1:13; 4:30).

- The Holy Spirit is our guarantee of salvation and eternal life with Him (see 2 Cor. 1:22; 5:4–5).

- The Holy Spirit enables us to obey the truth (see 1 Pet. 1:22).

- The Holy Spirit enables us to eagerly wait for the hope of righteousness by faith (see Gal. 5:5).

- The Holy Spirit is the One by whom we are baptized into the body of Christ (see 1 Cor. 12:13).

- The Holy Spirit gives us joy (see 1 Thess. 1:6–7).

- The Holy Spirit brings hope (see Rom. 14:17; 15:13).

- The Holy Spirit enables us to preach the gospel with power (see Rom. 1:4; 1 Thess. 1:5; 1 Pet. 1:12).

- The Holy Spirit guides us into all truth (see John 16:13).

*He who believes in Me, as the Scripture has said, out of his heart will flow rivers of living water.*
**John 7:38**

If you have any questions about the baptism with the Holy Spirit or the person or ministry of the Holy Spirit, write them below, and speak to your pastor or ministry leader about them.

## DAY 2: THE SPIRIT GIVES US HOPE IN TRIALS

There are many uncertainties in this life. Trials, heartaches, and tribulations are promised to us in the Word of God (see John 16:33; 2 Tim. 3:12), and they are often the very things God uses to touch and transform our lives. It is easy to understand, however, why people without hope in God are so filled with anxiety and despair and why people turn to unhealthy relationships and activities to fill that void. Without God's grace and Holy Spirit working in and through us to transform and empower us, we won't have the ability to persevere through this life. As we rest our hope fully upon the grace of Jesus Christ (see 1 Pet. 1:13) and walk in the power of the Spirit, we can have an eternal perspective that sees past the trials of this life and anchors us to the eternal hope that we have in Him.

The apostle Paul understood the need for spiritual empowerment as much as anyone in the Bible. During Paul's three missionary journeys, he encountered various trials and uncertainties as he set out to tell others about the eternal hope he had found in Jesus. Paul understood that God's Word is the one thing that always remains true, and he remembered the personal word God had spoken to him, promising him that he would get to Rome (see Acts 23:11). Because Paul knew that God would be true to His word, he was able to be "steadfast, immovable, always abounding in the work of the Lord," because he knew that his labor was "not in vain in the Lord" (1 Cor. 15:58).

In fact, when Paul was warned that chains and tribulations awaited him, his response in Acts 20:24 was,

"None of these things move me; nor do I count my life dear to myself, so that I may finish my race with joy, and the ministry which I received from the Lord Jesus, to testify to the gospel of the grace of God." Paul was a prime example of what it meant to be empowered by the Holy Spirit and to hold fast to the Word of the Lord. His hope was not in his circumstances or relationships here on earth but in the character, the promises, the Word, and the very person of God. As God touched Paul's heart, He also transformed Paul's perspective from a temporal to an eternal focus.

1. Look up 2 Corinthians 11:23–28, and record the constant trials Paul endured as he fulfilled his ministry to preach the gospel. As you record his trials, consider all Paul endured on a daily basis.

*I consider that the sufferings of this present time are not worthy to be compared with the glory which shall be revealed in us. For the earnest expectation of the creation eagerly waits for the revealing of the sons of God. . . . Not only that, but we also who have the firstfruits of the Spirit, even we ourselves groan within ourselves, eagerly waiting for the adoption, the redemption of our body. For we were saved in this hope, but hope that is seen is not hope; for why does one still hope for what he sees? But if we hope for what we do not see, we eagerly wait for it with perseverance.*

**Romans 8:18–25**

2. Do you wonder how Paul could say that the sufferings we encounter here on earth will not be worth comparing to the glory of heaven (see Rom. 8:18)? Look up 2 Corinthians 12:3–4, and record

what happened to Paul that made him able to make such a statement.

The apostle Paul was uniquely qualified to compare the sufferings of this world to the glory of eternal life because he had seen heaven with his own eyes. He understood the truth of Revelation 1:18, in which Jesus states, "I am the living one. I died, but look—I am alive forever and ever! And I hold the keys of death and the grave" (NLT). Paul knew that heaven was his real home, where he would live forever with Jesus when he took his last breath on this earth (see 2 Cor. 5:8). As Paul lived under the Lord's divine influence, overflowing with the Holy Spirit, he embraced this living hope of Jesus. Fixing his eyes on the upward call of God in Christ Jesus, Paul was able not only to persevere through the storms of his life but also to thrive and grow and know God more. The good news is that by the empowerment of His Spirit, we can do the same.

*Now, Lord, what do I wait for? My hope is in You.*

**Psalm 39:7**

## DAY 3: THE SPIRIT GIVES US HOPE IN
## AN ETERNAL PERSPECTIVE

Not only does the Holy Spirit strengthen us in the storms of life, but He also gives us hope as we learn to see things through an eternal perspective. Hope is one of the most powerful concepts in the life of a believer. Hope strengthens us, calms our fears, gives us courage, and says to us, "What you see with your eyes is not all there is." Like Paul, Abraham placed his hope in God alone, and his testimony is a beautiful example of how the Holy Spirit can give us hope in God that produces within us an eternal point of view.

When God asked Abraham to sacrifice his son Isaac, Abraham had already had enough experience with God to know that the Lord would fulfill His word. Hebrews 11:17–19 says that "by faith Abraham, when he was tested, offered up Isaac, and he who had received the promises offered up his only begotten son, of whom it was said, 'In Isaac your seed shall be called,' concluding that God was able to raise him up, even from the dead."

Isaac was the fulfillment of one promise in God's bigger plan to bless the nations. In Genesis 12:2–3 God had promised Abraham, "I will make you a great nation; I will bless you and make your name great; and you shall be a blessing. I will bless those who bless you, . . . and in you all the families of the earth shall be blessed." Abraham was willing to sacrifice Isaac because he believed that God would still fulfill His promise for the nations. His radical hope came from his rock-solid faith that God was even able to raise Isaac from the dead to fulfill His promise if needed. Abraham didn't have the full picture of God's plan, but because he walked with God, trusting in His character, he had the strength and confidence to do what God asked of him. He had seen God's faithfulness in the past, so he was able to look forward with hope.

Hope in God's unchanging character empowered Paul's endurance as well. Paul knew, as Abraham had, that he did not belong in this world; he was just passing through to an eternal home. Paul expressed this idea in 2 Corinthians 5:1 when he stated, "We know that if our earthly house, this tent [the physical body], is destroyed, we have a building from God, a house not made with hands, eternal in the heavens." Paul continued in verse 8, "We are confident, yes, well pleased rather to be absent from the body and to be present with the Lord." Likewise, Hebrews 11:13–16 goes on to say that those who walked in faith "confessed that they were strangers and pilgrims on the earth," desiring "a better, that is, a heavenly country. Therefore God is not ashamed to be called their God, for He has prepared a city for them." These truths echo the words of Jesus, who tells us in John 14:1–3,

> Let not your heart be troubled; you believe in God, believe also in Me. In My Father's house are many mansions; if it were not so, I would have told you. I go to prepare a place for you. And if I go and prepare a place for you, I will come again and receive you to Myself; that where I am, there you may be also.

As children of God, our citizenship is in heaven. Heaven is our real home; we are just passing through this world with the glorious opportunity to point others to God, sharing the eternal hope we have found in Him. Faith in God brings the "living hope" that Peter spoke of in 1 Peter 1:3–5, hope that will carry us beyond any despair. The assurance of God's presence with us here on earth each and every day and the hope of being in His presence for all eternity enable us to endure the hardships, pain, storms, and weariness of this life and allow us to be lights, causing others to ask the reason for the hope that is in us (see 1 Pet. 3:15).

This hope does not come naturally, especially when our world seems to be crumbling around us, but it is available to us through the Holy Spirit, who lives and works within us: "May the God of hope fill you with all joy and peace in believing, that you may abound in hope by the power of the Holy Spirit" (Rom. 15:13).

1. What are your expectations for your life?

2. How do your expectations line up with the Word of God?

*Be of good courage, and He shall strengthen your heart, all you who hope in the LORD.*

Psalm 31:24

3. What did Peter mean when he referenced a "living hope" in 1 Peter 1:3–5?

4. How can you have an eternal perspective? Who is the source of all hope?

A. Why is an eternal perspective important in the life of a believer?

B. How does being happy here on earth compare to the joy found in an eternal perspective?

*May our Lord Jesus Christ Himself, and our God and Father, who has loved us and given us everlasting consolation and good hope by grace, comfort your hearts and establish you in every good word and work.*

**2 Thessalonians 2:16–17**

## DAY 4: THE SPIRIT GIVES US HOPE IN ABIDING

To abide in Christ means to remain under His lordship by the help of the Holy Spirit.

In John 15:5 Jesus presented the idea of abiding when He likened Himself to a grapevine and believers to its branches, saying, "Abide in Me, and I in you. As the branch cannot bear fruit of itself, unless it abides in the vine, neither can you, unless you abide in Me." This illustrates the spiritual intimacy that exists between Christians and Jesus Christ. How do we know if we are abiding in Christ? First John 4:13 tells us: "By this we know that we abide in Him, and He in us, because He has given us of His Spirit."

All spiritual life and growth begin with the abiding presence of God by His Spirit. Peter tells us in 2 Peter 1:3–4 that "His divine power has given to us all things that pertain to life and godliness, through the knowledge of Him who called us by glory and virtue, by which have been given to us exceedingly great and precious promises, that through these you may be partakers of the divine nature." This is where we see the extent of the intimate relationship with God that He has provided to us by His new covenant of grace. At salvation we did not merely come near to Christ, nor did He simply draw close to us; rather we now live in Him, and He lives in us. We live by being in Christ, being united with Him, and drawing our spiritual life from Him. Consequently, He lives in us and desires to express His life through us as we seek to grow in the grace and knowledge of Him.

> *I have one desire now: to live a life of reckless abandon for the Lord, putting all my energy and strength into it.*
>
> **Elisabeth Elliot**

To abide in Christ is to abide in His Word. Throughout our study we have seen the importance and benefits of knowing the names of God, but it is also vital for us to understand the priority God places upon the entirety of His Word. In Psalm 138:2 the psalmist says to the Lord, "You have magnified Your word above all Your name." God has given us His precious Word to enable and encourage us to "grow in the grace and knowledge of our Lord and Savior Jesus Christ" (2 Pet. 3:18).

We must not neglect the Word of God; it is our source of spiritual nourishment, containing all we need to know about who God is, His character and attributes, and His promises. As you move on from this study, remember that dark times are promised to come (see John 16:33), and while it may seem at times that there is no way out, God's Word reminds us that with Him and in Him, there is always hope. As the psalmist states in Psalm 119:114, "You are my hiding place and my shield; I hope in Your word."

1. Read the entirety of Psalm 119, and notice the prominence of the Word of God mentioned throughout it.

   A. Make a list of the benefits you see regarding the Word of God for your life. How many can you find?

B. Which ones mean the most to you, and why?

Of course, we can abide in Christ only by the power of the Holy Spirit within us. In fact, we can do nothing apart from the abiding presence of the Spirit. As Jesus was leaving His disciples, soon to return to the Father, He comforted His followers by saying, "I will not leave you orphans; I will come to you. A little while longer and the world will see Me no more, but you will see Me. Because I live, you will live also" (John 14:18–19). On the day of Pentecost, the Holy Spirit was poured forth in fullness and power, and today He makes abiding in Jesus possible to all His followers. As we abide in Him, lasting fruit will be produced through us to the glory of God.

For Christ to live in us and for us to live in Him, all we must do is seek the life He offers. Romans 8:11 tells us, "He who raised Christ from the dead will also give life to your mortal bodies through His Spirit who dwells in you." Ask the Lord to help you see that the abiding life is as simple as eating and drinking. As you trust food and drink for your daily physical life, tell Jesus that you want to trust Him for your spiritual life; it's as simple as asking, receiving, and then continuing in Him.

2. Read John 15:1–17 below.

I am the true vine, and My Father is the vinedresser. Every branch in Me that does not bear fruit He takes away; and every branch that bears fruit He prunes, that it may bear more fruit. You are already clean because of the word which I have spoken to you. Abide in Me, and I in you. As the branch cannot bear fruit of itself, unless it abides in the vine, neither can you, unless you abide in Me.

I am the vine, you are the branches. He who abides in Me, and I in him, bears much fruit; for without Me you can do nothing. If anyone does not abide in Me, he is cast out as a branch and is withered; and they gather them and throw them into the fire, and they are burned. If you abide in Me, and My words abide in you, you will ask what you desire, and it shall be done for you. By this My Father is glorified, that you bear much fruit; so you will be My disciples. As the Father loved Me, I also have loved you; abide in My love. If you keep My commandments, you will abide in

*Do you want more and more of God's kindness and peace? Then learn to know him better and better. For as you know him better, he will give you, through his great power, everything you need for living a truly good life: he even shares his own glory and his own goodness with us! And by that same mighty power he has given us all the other rich and wonderful blessings he promised; for instance, the promise to save us from the lust and rottenness all around us, and to give us his own character.*

**2 Peter 1:2–4, TLB**

My love, just as I have kept My Father's commandments and abide in His love.

These things I have spoken to you, that My joy may remain in you, and that your joy may be full. This is My commandment, that you love one another as I have loved you. Greater love has no one than this, than to lay down one's life for his friends. You are My friends if you do whatever I command you. No longer do I call you servants, for a servant does not know what his master is doing; but I have called you friends, for all things that I heard from My Father I have made known to you. You did not choose Me, but I chose you and appointed you that you should go and bear fruit, and that your fruit should remain, that whatever you ask the Father in My name He may give you. These things I command you, that you love one another.

*Brethren, I do not count myself to have apprehended; but one thing I do, forgetting those things which are behind and reaching forward to those things which are ahead, I press toward the goal for the prize of the upward call of God in Christ Jesus.*

**Philippians 3:13–14**

Respond to what you just read by writing in your own words what gives you hope to move forward.

## DAY 5: THE NAMES OF GOD: LOOKING TO JESUS

One final thing that we must understand about the Holy Spirit is that He never draws attention to Himself. He always and ever points men and women to Jesus Christ. This is exactly what Jesus told His disciples that the Spirit would do: "When He, the Spirit of truth, has come, He will guide you into all truth; for He will not speak on His own authority, but whatever He hears He will speak; and He will tell you things to come. *He will glorify Me,* for He will take of what is Mine and declare it to you" (John 16:13–14).

As we come to the final lesson of this study, we will review the names of God that we have covered throughout *Touched and Transformed.* As you look at each name and are reminded of the character and promises of God that it represents, remember that they also point to Jesus Christ, the Word. Take the time to meditate on the character traits of God represented in each name and highlight the attributes of God that you need to be reminded of today.

1. *Elohim* (see Gen. 1:1)

   A. What character trait of God do you understand from this name?

B. What does the name *Elohim* mean in your life today?

2. *El Elyon* (see Dan. 4:34–37)

   A. What character trait of God do you understand from this name?

   B. What does the name *El Elyon* mean in your life today?

3. *El Shaddai* (see Gen. 17:1; John 10:7–9)

   A. What character trait of God do you understand from this name?

  B. What does the name *El Shaddai* mean in your life today?

4. *Jehovah Tsidqenuw* (see Jer. 23:6)

  A. What character trait of God do you understand from this name?

  B. What does the name *Jehovah Tsidqenuw* mean in your life today?

5. *El Nasa* (see Ps. 99:8)

  A. What character trait of God do you understand from this name?

B. What does the name *El Nasa* mean in your life today?

6. *El Ahava* (see Deut. 23:5)

A. What character trait of God do you understand from this name?

B. What does the name *El Ahava* mean in your life today?

7. *Jehovah Rapha* (see Exod. 15:26)

A. What character trait of God do you understand from this name?

B. What does the name *Jehovah Rapha* mean in your life today?

8. *Jehovah Yireh* (see Gen. 22:14)

A. What character trait of God do you understand from this name?

B. What does the name *Jehovah Yireh* mean in your life today?

9. *El Kanna* (see Exod. 20:4–5)

A. What character trait of God do you understand from this name?

B. What does the name *El Kanna* mean in your life today?

10. *Adonai/Yahweh/Jehovah*/I Am (see Exod. 3:14–15)

A. What character trait of God do you understand from this name?

B. What does the name *Adonai/Yahweh/Jehovah*/I Am mean in your life today?

11. *El Roi* (see Gen. 16:13)

A. What character trait of God do you understand from this name?

B. What does the name *El Roi* mean in your life today?

12. *Jehovah Shammah* (see Ezek. 48:35)

A. What character trait of God do you understand from this name?

B. What does the name *Jehovah Shammah* mean in your life today?

13. *Jehovah Sabaoth* (see 1 Sam. 17:45)

A. What character trait of God do you understand from this name?

B. What does the name *Jehovah Sabaoth* mean in your life today?

*Since we are surrounded by so great a cloud of witnesses, let us lay aside every weight, and the sin which so easily ensnares us, and let us run with endurance the race that is set before us, looking unto Jesus, the author and finisher of our faith, who for the joy that was set before Him endured the cross, despising the shame, and has sat down at the right hand of the throne of God.*

**Hebrews 12:1–2**

14. *Jehovah Shalom* (see Judg. 6:24)

A. What character trait of God do you understand from this name?

B. What does the name *Jehovah Shalom* mean in your life today?

15. Write a prayer calling upon the names and character of God as it pertains to your situation.

Jesus alone is our hope. He came the first time as the sinless, spotless Lamb of God who took all our sin upon Himself, and one day He will come again as the conquering King, "that at the name of Jesus every knee should bow, of those in heaven, and of those on earth, and of those under the earth, and that every tongue should confess that Jesus Christ is Lord, to the glory of God the Father" (Phil. 2:10–11). He is our creator, sustainer, peace, victory, shepherd, righteousness, sanctification, rock, refuge, defense, provider, and healer. He is everlasting, ever present, ever seeing, the lover of our souls, and jealous for us. He is merciful, He is living water, He is the bread of life. He is our everything.

*Some trust in chariots, and some in horses; but we will remember the name of the LORD our God.*

**Psalm 20:7**

In a world of increasing despair and hopelessness, it is easy for us to focus on the uncertainties, misery, hatred, problems, and disasters in the world around us. Instead, by the power of the Holy Spirit within us, we must look to Jesus and the forgiveness, freedom, and favor He offers that make our trials seem small; we must focus on the eternal hope that has been given to us; we must abide in Christ as we abide in His Word. Only the Lord Jesus Christ makes sense of the senseless and gives hope to the hopeless.

God wants to use us in the lives of others, and we have never had a better opportunity than now to give others a reason for the hope in our own hearts.

# AFTERWORD

Going through this study, or any study or program, for that matter, is not a cure-all for your life. Jesus alone is your cure. It is important to go before the Lord continually in dependence upon Him, seeking His transforming touch in every aspect of your life as you grow in your relationship with Him. Spending time with Jesus in His Word and in dependence upon the Holy Spirit should not stop when you complete these chapters.

Healing is not about a person you can meet with, a book you can read, or a Bible study you can complete. It is about surrendering your life to Jesus, the author and finisher of your faith (see Heb. 12:2). People will let you down and disappoint you, but as you look to Jesus and His Word, continually allowing the Holy Spirit to fill you, He will never disappoint. Dark seasons will come, but the Son will rise; He is with you through it all, for you are His, and He has redeemed you (see Isa. 43:1). You can completely rest in Him, for He "will never leave you nor forsake you" (Heb. 13:5). Once you realize all that Jesus has done and will continue to do for you, God's glory will shine through your life to all around you.

Please call your church and ask to speak to a pastor or ministry leader, and let them know that you just completed this study and would like to get involved in a Bible study or a discipleship class. Ask them to pray with you so that you can continue to look to Jesus to be your all in all, "being confident of this very thing, that He who has begun a good

> *God will allow us to follow self-help, self-improvement programs until we have tried them all, until we finally come to the honest confession, "I can't do it. I can't be righteous in my own strength!" It is then, when we admit our utter powerlessness, that we find hope. For it is then when the Lord intervenes to do a work that we could not do for ourselves.*
>
> Chuck Smith

work in you will complete it until the day of Jesus Christ" (Phil. 1:6). If you do not have a church, I encourage you to find a Bible-teaching church where you can continue in fellowship and grow in your relationship with Jesus. The writer of Hebrews exhorts believers, "Let us consider one another in order to stir up love and good works, not forsaking the assembling of ourselves together, as is the manner of some, but exhorting one another, and so much the more as you see the Day approaching" (Heb. 10:24–25).

Just as the Lord was willing to touch and heal the leper (see Matt. 8:3), so He is willing to continuously touch your life, today and every day, bringing to you His healing and transformation. "May God himself, the God of peace, sanctify you through and through. May your whole spirit, soul and body be kept blameless at the coming of our Lord Jesus Christ. The one who calls you is faithful, and *he will do it*" (1 Thess. 5:23–24, NIV). May the Lord bless you as you continue to seek His face and grow in His grace and knowledge, getting to know Him in order to make Him known!

*We see that when God moves among His people in revival, whether it's one heart or many hearts, in your church or your home or your community, that unbelievers are compelled to take God seriously. When the people of God are living as the people of God, when they're experiencing the fullness of all God intended for them, when they've been set free from their captivity, then the unbelieving world is compelled to take notice and compelled to take God seriously. "Then they said among the nations, 'The Lord has done great things for them.'"*

**Nancy DeMoss Wolgemuth**

*You will keep him in perfect peace, whose mind is stayed on You, because he trusts in You.*

**Isaiah 26:3**

# NOTES

**WEEK 1: TOUCHED AND TRANSFORMED—HEALING IN JESUS**

1. A. W. Tozer, *The Root of the Righteous* (Harrisburg, PA: Christian Publications, 1986), 9.

2. Tozer, *Evenings with Tozer: Daily Devotional Readings* (Chicago: Moody, 2015), 112.

**WEEK 3: TOUCHED AND TRANSFORMED BY HIS LOVE**

1. Spiros Zodhiates, *The Complete Word Study Dictionary: New Testament* (Chattanooga, TN: AMG, 1993), 771.

**WEEK 4: TOUCHED AND TRANSFORMED IN BROKENNESS**

1. Victor Marx, *The Victor Marx Story: With God, All Things Are Possible* (Murrieta, CA: Onesimus, 2013), victormarx.com/two-roads-which-one-will-you-choose/.

# JOURNAL

# JOURNAL

# JOURNAL

# JOURNAL

# JOURNAL

# JOURNAL

# JOURNAL

# JOURNAL

# JOURNAL

# JOURNAL

# JOURNAL

# JOURNAL